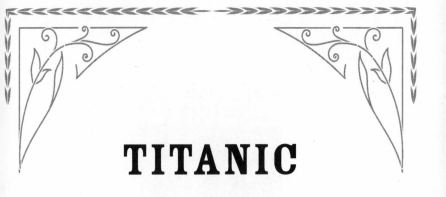

TITANIC

NICOLA PIERCE

published her first book, *Spirit of the Titanic*, to rave
reviews and five printings within its first twelve
months. *City of Fate*, her second book transported
the reader deep into the Russian city of Stalingrad
during the Second World War. *Behind the Walls*, a rich
emotional novel set in the besieged city of Derry in
1689 was followed with a companion novel, *Kings of
the Boyne*, also set in the seventeenth century during a
defining moment in Irish history.

To read more about Nicola, go to her web page, www.
nicolapierce.com. To understand her connection to,
and research on, *Titanic*, see the
Author's Note on pages 8–9 of this book.

TITANIC

TRUE STORIES OF

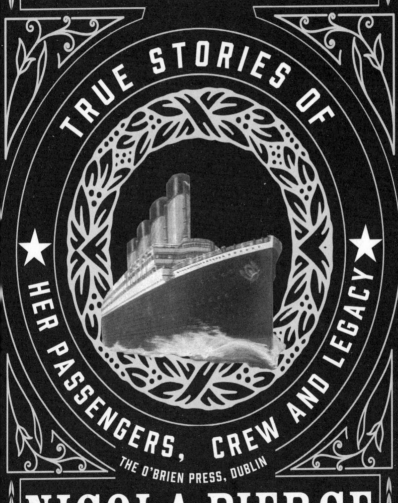

HER PASSENGERS, CREW AND LEGACY

THE O'BRIEN PRESS, DUBLIN

NICOLA PIERCE

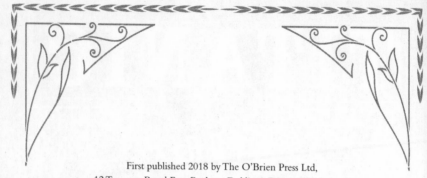

First published 2018 by The O'Brien Press Ltd,
12 Terenure Road East, Rathgar, Dublin 6, D06 HD27, Ireland.
Tel: +353 1 4923333; Fax: +353 1 4922777
E-mail: books@obrien.ie; Website: www.obrien.ie
The O'Brien Press is a member of Publishing Ireland.
Reprinted 2019.

ISBN: 978-1-84717-947-0

3 5 7 9 10 8 6 4 2
20 22 21 19

Printed and bound by Gutenberg Press, Malta.
The paper in this book is produced using pulp from managed forests.

Published in
DUBLIN
UNESCO
City of Literature

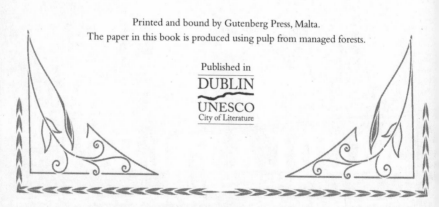

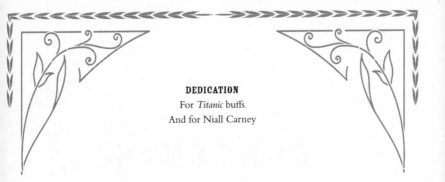

DEDICATION

For *Titanic* buffs
And for Niall Carney

ACKNOWLEDGEMENTS

The author would like to extend her gratitude to the following for assistance and their
generosity in research: *Titanic* historians and authors Randy Bryan Bigham,
Steve Hall and Bill Wormstedt, Straus Historical Society (Executive Director Joan Adler),
Southampton FC (Official Historian to SFC, Duncan Holley), Julie Stoner at the Library
of Congress and Zoe Rainey who kindly checked out graveyards for me on her
New York holiday.

I also wish to thank The O'Brien Press for asking me to write this book. As always, I must
thank my tireless editor, Susan Houlden, for all her help and encouragement. I depend on
her sharing my passions, book to book, and she never fails me.
The fact that this book looks good is absolutely nothing to do with me; once again I'm
grateful for the artist that is Emma Byrne. I can only hope the book is as good as it looks.
Also, I hasten to add, any mistakes are entirely mine.

CONTENTS

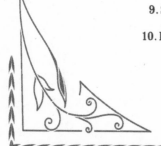

AUTHOR'S NOTE

RMS *Titanic* changed my life with the release of my children's novel *Spirit of the Titanic*. The tragedy is narrated by the spirit of the first victim associated with *Titanic*, a fifteen-year-old catch-boy, or junior riveter, Samuel Joseph Scott who was working on the building of the great ship in the Harland & Wolff shipyard. On 20 April 1910, Samuel fell twenty-three feet to his death from a ladder propped against the side of the ship. I had no idea that the research I had undertaken for the novel and the novel itself would result in my spending the next six years crisscrossing the island of Ireland, including a jaunt to the Irish college in Paris, talking to students of all ages, teachers, librarians and parents about *Titanic*. I have been ambushed by four-year-olds determined to show me their *Titanic* portraits, while older and elderly *Titanic* enthusiasts have shared their own research and connections with me.

Over the years, many theories have been explored as to the cause of the sinking, including that of a fire in Boiler Room 6. During my talks, I have been asked a lot of questions about the ship, some I could answer and some I could not. My publisher wanted an accessible, affordable history book, which presented me with a huge challenge as I sifted through the mound of information available, needing to cram in as much as I could, in as few words as possible. Admittedly, some of the stories will be familiar; however, I learned a lot during the research and I hope that the reader might share my experience.

Titanic's wreck still lies in two sections on the floor of the Atlantic Ocean, while over in China a replica is being built at the Romandisea Seven Star International Cultural Tourism Resort. Their Facebook page already has over 900,000 followers, who avidly comment on the new build via the regularly updated photographs.

Over a century after its fateful journey to the bottom of the sea, this ship, her crew and passengers continue to enthral young and old.

Nicola Pierce

Titanic's gigantic propellers.

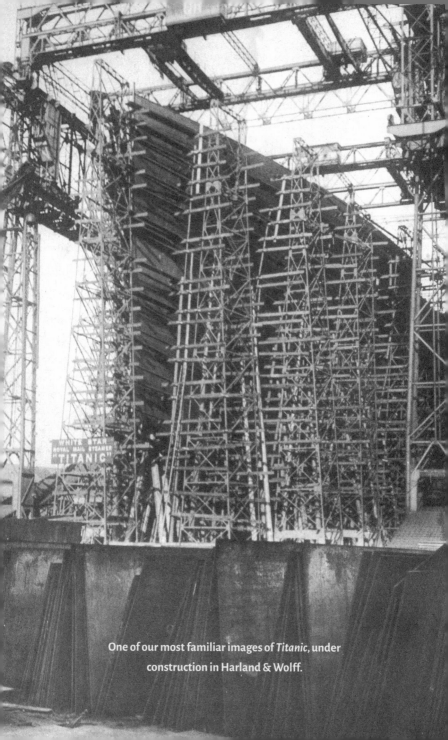

One of our most familiar images of *Titanic*, under construction in Harland & Wolff.

TITANIC

HOW IT ALL BEGAN

Out on the seas in the early years of the twentieth century the Cunard Line held supreme, with the much-loved ships, *Lusitania* and *Mauretania*, the biggest, fastest and most lavishly built ships the world had ever seen. In 1907 the number of immigrants travelling to a new life in America totalled a new high at 1.25 million.

There was much money to be made and stiff competition to stir ambition into being. In 1907, Mr Joseph Bruce Ismay, chairman of the White Star Line, and his wife, Florence, were invited to dinner at Downshire House, the London home of Lord Pirrie, chairman of Belfast's Harland & Wolff shipyard. We may assume that the premise of this dinner was to initiate changes that would prove beneficial to both companies.

Bruce Ismay was also president and managing director of IMM (International Mercantile Marine Company), the American holding company that had bought the shipping White Star Line in 1902.

The entrepreneurial swagger behind the IMM was undoubtedly John Pierpoint (JP) Morgan, the crusading powerhouse whose

Nobody could have guessed that *Titanic* was leaving Belfast behind forever.

nose for profit had brought him to the water's edge. As an American, he was not allowed to own British ships, but there was nothing to prevent his holding company from owning the company that owned the British ships. In typical fashion, Morgan wished to buy out and thus dominate the relatively new world of the transatlantic liner. Along with White Star Line, he had briefly attempted to buy the Cunard Line but was thwarted by the British government who feared an American monopoly of the North Atlantic trade.

Today, 24 Belgrave Square, the Greco-Roman-styled mansion formerly known as Downshire House, is home to the Spanish

Embassy. However, it is far more famous for that 1907 dinner party, during which the two esteemed chairmen, Lord Pirrie and Bruce Ismay, dreamt up *Titanic* and her sisters. The future of sea travel was in their hands and what they would conceive was undoubtedly a fine testament to the mutually beneficial relationship between a British shipping line and a Belfast ship-building company.

Three years later, an article in the *Belfast News Letter* described this relationship as 'one of the most interesting chapters in the history of our ship-building industry'.

It was surely inevitable that Ismay, with IMM funding, and Pirrie would look to breach Cunard's superiority and the answer was as obvious as it was simple: White Star Line needed new ships and these new ships needed to exceed the Cunard liners in size, speed and luxury. The two men went to work that very evening, making sketches and bestowing names that announced a new type of ship on the horizon: *Olympic*, *Titanic* and *Gigantic*. Of course, the consequences of that conversation would have huge financial requirements; that is, those three ships could only happen thanks to White Star Line's access to the considerable resources of the IMM.

NOBODY COULD HAVE GUESSED THAT *TITANIC* WAS LEAVING BELFAST BEHIND FOREVER.

Left: No image of *Titanic*'s Grand Staircase is
known to exist. Pictured here the Grand Staircase
in *Olympic* was of the same design; a replica of
the one in *Titanic* can be seen at Titanic Belfast.

JP Morgan had made his desires clear, telling Ismay to 'build me
the finest vessels afloat', and that is exactly what he got, not three
years later, with *Olympic*'s launch on 20 October 1910, followed
closely by her sister *Titanic*'s on 31 May 1911. *Gigantic* would
be finally launched as *Britannic*, on 26 February 1914, to a very
different world.

In a way, *Titanic* was initially in her elder sister's shadow, not
receiving half the fanfare that had been afforded to the first of the
White Star Line wonder ships but that would change. Made in
the image of *Olympic*, *Titanic* was just that bit heavier at 46,328
tonnes to *Olympic*'s 45,324, because the forward half of *Titanic*'s A
deck promenade was enclosed by a steel screen with sliding windows while *Olympic*'s promenade deck was completely open to the
elements.

Due to her spacious A deck promenade, *Olympic*'s wealthier passengers had no need for the first-class promenades on B deck and,
consequently, the B deck first-class promenades did not appear on
Titanic. Instead, Thomas Andrews used the space to build extra,
and enlarged, first-class suites. Furthermore, he made a tasteful
extension to the À la Carte Restaurant in the form of the Café
Parisien. Resembling a Parisian street café, this had never been
seen on a British ship before. Passengers could order a meal from
the restaurant and, if they so wished, take it in the café, sitting in

front of its large windows to enjoy the waterscape as they ate. Weather permitting, the windows could be rolled down, allowing passengers to feel like they were eating outside a café, another first for sea-faring passengers. Thomas Andrews was breaking new ground with *Titanic* and one can only wonder what he might have done with *Britannic*. Thanks to the café's popularity, particularly with the younger passengers, *Olympic* would later receive her own Café Parisien.

Another *Titanic* specification was a reception area for the restaurant that was added in B deck, behind the Grand Staircase, while the main reception room on D deck was also enlarged. The two deluxe parlour suites on B deck were given their own promenades and there were more first-class gangway entrances on B deck too.

A ship full of steerage passengers would certainly pay its way, but the real money was to be made from the likes of the Astors, Guggenheims and their peers. *Titanic's* innovative chief designer ensured his ship was the biggest and most luxurious ever to put to sea, and the rich flocked to board her in April 1912.

How exciting it must have been, on leaving Queenstown behind, to know that there would be no more stops, that all passengers and bags of mail were safely onboard and that, at long last, they were on their way to New York.

In many ways, what happened next is still somewhat unbelievable.

TITANIC TIMELINE

1908
16 December: *Olympic*'s keel is laid and construction begins.

1909
31 March: *Titanic*'s keel is laid and construction begins.

1910
16 April: *Titanic*'s frame is completed.
20 April: Catch-boy Samuel Joseph Scott in fatal fall from side of ship.
19 October: *Titanic*'s plating is completed.

1911
31 May: *Titanic* is launched just after midday in front of 100,000 people.
14 June: *Olympic* commences her maiden voyage.
20 September: *Olympic* collides with HMS *Hawke*, delaying *Titanic*'s completion.
30 November: *Britannic*'s keel is laid and construction begins.

1912
January: Lifeboats are fitted on *Titanic*.
31 March: Construction of *Titanic* is completed.
3 February: *Titanic* captured on news reel, entering the dry dock.

2 April: Following successful sea trials Francis Carruthers signs the Certificate of Sea-Worthiness, valid for one year, and *Titanic* leaves Belfast forever.
3 April: *Titanic* docks in Southampton.
10 April: *Titanic* leaves Southampton and sails to Cherbourg.
11 April: *Titanic* docks at Roches Point, off the coast of Queenstown, to pick up her final passengers and post bags. Two hours later she leaves for New York.
14 April: At 11.40pm, four days into her first and only voyage, *Titanic* strikes an iceberg about 375 miles south of Newfoundland.
15 April: At 2.17am, the last message is transmitted from the *Titanic* before her final plunge at 2.20am. A little over 700 passengers, out of an approximate 2,223 on board, make it safely into lifeboats.
Just after 4am, RMS *Carpathia* arrives to rescue the survivors.

1985
1 September: *Titanic* is sighted, after a disappearance of 73 years, when Robert Ballard discovers her wreck, torn in two, on the Atlantic Ocean floor.

The Great Titanic Disaster

Wireless Operator on Shipboard receiving Distress Call
Life boats bringing Titanic's Survivors to the Carpathia
Capt. Smith of the Titanic

Life boat Drill   The lost Liner

Above: The world was shocked as news spread of *Titanic*'s fate.

Opposite top: A sideroom of *Titanic*'s opulent first-class dining room, the largest room on any ship at the time.

Opposite bottom: Pictured is *Olympic*'s first-class smoking room, identical to *Titanic*'s and designed as a gentlemen's club with mahogany panelling

Captain Edward John Smith with his *Titanic* officers, only four of whom would survive *Titanic*'s maiden voyage.

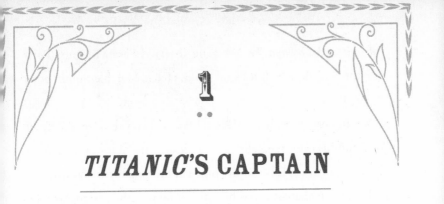

TITANIC'S CAPTAIN

I n his photographs, Edward John Smith looks exactly like a seafaring captain of old with his solid figure, white hair and weathered face complemented by a trim beard. He is forever ingrained in our minds as 'the captain of the *Titanic*' since, to the author's knowledge, no photographs exist in the public domain showing him in civilian clothes.

Hanley, in the English Staffordshire town of Stoke-on-Trent, was the land-locked town of his birth and childhood, and is many miles from the sea. He was named after his father, Edward, who was a potter before going into retail and buying a shop with his wife, Catherine. According to an old trade journal from 1893, the prosperous Hanley was the capital of the potteries.

Captain Smith embraced his destiny at an early age. Leaving school at thirteen, he made his way to Liverpool and got himself an apprenticeship with the Gibson shipping line before joining White Star in 1880. Seven years later, at the age of 37, he earned his first command and, on his way to captaining *Titanic* in 1912, took the helm of many ships including the *Majestic*, the *Baltic*, the

Adriatic and *Olympic*. In 1887, he married Sarah Eleanor Pennington and they had just one child, Helen Melville Smith, born in 1898.

Smith served with the British Royal Navy, during the Boer War, and his calm reliability earned him a medal for bravery from the hand of King Edward VII himself. Presumably it was this sort of behaviour that attracted his fans, those wealthy passengers who preferred to sail on his ship over any other White Star captain's, leading to his nickname, 'Millionaire's Captain'. However else they may have felt about the number of funnels or, indeed, lifeboats, most of the first-class passengers would have been reassured by the very fact that they were on Captain Smith's ship. He was as popular with the men who worked with him, his crew, who called him 'EJ', although only when he was out of earshot. As White Star Line's most popular officer and, also, the highest paid, with an annual salary of £1,250, it was no surprise that he would be asked to take the brand new, biggest ship in the world out on her maiden voyage.

Walter Lord, in his book *A Night to Remember*, writes that the sixty-two-year-old captain had been about to retire but boarded *Titanic* to fulfil a final request from White Star Line. Some dispute that fact today; however, it certainly adds pathos to his story. In every way possible, this was to be Captain Smith's final journey.

After his death, an old Hanley school friend, William Jones, gave an account of the boy, Ted Smith, who would go on to become one of the world's most famous captains. William Jones declared that Smith had died exactly as he would have wished, standing on the bridge of his ship thus ensuring that he went down with her because that was typical of the boy he described as brave, kind and generous.

Perhaps it is only right and natural that the exact fate of *Titanic*'s captain remains a mystery, thanks to several conflicting stories from survivors who claimed the last sighting of him. An American passenger, George Brereton (sometimes listed as G.A. Braden) was in the water and saw Captain Smith standing alone on *Titanic*. He watched a wave knock the captain off his feet but Smith stood up once more as the ship sank, only to be knocked over by a second wave. Brereton did not see him again. Entrée cook Isaac Maynard, who was standing on the back of the overturned Collapsible B, spotted the captain in the water and, with his fellow passengers, tried to pull him aboard but the captain slipped off again. As far as Fireman Harry Senior was concerned, the captain did not slip but purposely let go to follow his ship.

Meanwhile, an interview appeared in the *Daily Sketch* newspaper on 30 April 1912 with Mr George Standing, a friend of Charles Williams, the squash player who survived the sinking. Mr Standing repeated what Charles told him, which was that he saw Captain Smith in the water with a baby. A lifeboat went to his rescue and the captain handed over the child but refused to get into the boat. Instead, he asked the whereabouts of First Officer Murdoch and, on hearing that Murdock was dead, Captain Smith removed his life jacket and disappeared under the water, never to be seen again.

Other versions have him shouting at those in the lifeboat, 'Be brave, be British,' before disappearing. There was outrage when a completely different story appeared in some newspapers. Who knows who started the rumour but presumably *someone* told *someone else* that Captain Smith committed suicide, shooting himself in the head even before the lifeboats were released. The *London Daily Telegraph*, in its 20 April edition, surmised that the rumour began after several survivors attested to hearing revolver shots on *Titanic*'s deck. Today it is believed that the gun belonged to Fifth Officer Lowe, who fired his weapon, away from the passengers, as a warning to some men attempting to rush the lifeboats. The *Telegraph* journalist interviewed many of the survivors, including the crew, and the story of Captain Smith's suicide was vigorously rejected by one and all. He was told repeatedly that the captain remained on *Titanic*'s bridge until she sank and then was briefly seen in the water refusing to be saved. His body was never recovered. His memorial service was held in St Mark's Church, Shelton, Hanley, on 5 May 1912.

Captain Smith was exonerated of all blame in the investigations into the sinking. Questions were raised as to whether all the warnings about icebergs that were received by *Titanic* on 14 April were passed on to the captain. The only person who would have known one way or another was wireless operator Jack Phillips, who did not survive the tragedy. Lord Mersey, who led the British Wreck Commissioner's Inquiry, surmised that Captain Smith had made a mistake in not reducing *Titanic*'s speed or posting extra look-outs, but it was understandable since he was travelling a well-worn route used by many passenger ships over the previous twenty-five years, who all would have maintained speed, trusting to a sharp lookout to spot danger in time. Captain Smith was merely following suit and, therefore, could not be accused of negligence.

After the sinking Eleanor, his widow, wrote a note which was put up outside the White Star offices in Southampton:

To my poor fellow sufferers, my heart overflows with grief for you all and is laden with sorrow that you are weighed down with this terrible burden that has been thrust upon us. May God be with us and comfort us all.
Yours in sympathy,
Eleanor Smith

His death was not the only tragedy to befall the family. Eleanor died after being knocked down by a London taxi in 1931. Helen, their daughter, who was sometimes known as Mel, died in 1973, having buried two husbands and her only two children. Her first marriage was to Captain John Gilbertson and, when he died, she married Sidney Russell-Cooke in 1922. The following year, she gave birth to twins Simon and Priscilla. She was widowed a second time, in 1930, when Sidney accidentally shot himself in the stomach whilst cleaning his rifle. Simon joined the RAF in 1941 and died in action in 1944. Priscilla married a lawyer in 1946 but

NO ONE DIED AND EVEN THE PARROT WAS SAVED.

died childless a year later from polio and, therefore, there are no direct descendants of Captain Smith today.

A statue of Captain Smith was unveiled on 29 July 1914, in Beacon Park, Lichfield, Staffordshire, which was sculpted by Kathleen Scott, wife of Antarctic explorer, Captain Robert Falcon Scott. Coincidentally, on 22 February 1915, Madame Tussaud's, in London, launched their latest model, a waxwork of Captain Robert Falcon Scott, that stood right next to their model of Captain Edward John Smith. The two men had died in 1912, at the peak of their chosen professions, about two weeks apart, in freezing temperatures and far from home. Unfortunately, both figures were lost to a fire that blazed its way through the museum on 18 March 1925 and took an hour and a half to extinguish. No one died and even the parrot was saved. Firemen were unsure whether the bird was real or wax but, once out in the fresh air, it soon revived and informed onlookers that, 'This was a rotten business.'

2

TITANIC'S SISTERS AND THEIR DISASTERS

RMS OLYMPIC (ROYAL MAIL SHIP) (1908–1935)

*O**lympic's* keel was laid on 16 December 1908 in shipyard No. 400. Her younger sister would be constructed next door at 401. Begun and completed before *Titanic*, *Olympic* was temporarily the biggest and grandest ship in the world.

At 4.30pm, on the day of *Titanic's* launch, 31 May 1911, *Olympic* set sail for Liverpool under the command of Captain Edward John Smith with passengers including J Bruce Ismay, Chairman and Managing Director of White Star Line, and Thomas Andrews of Harland and Wolff, and also many of the crew who would later serve on *Titanic*. After Liverpool, she made her way to Southampton, from where she set out, on 14 June, on her maiden voyage to New York. The journey took 5 days, 16 hours and 42 minutes with an average speed of 21.7 knots.

A large crowd came out to welcome the biggest ship in the world to New York. There was a minor setback, however, when the tug boat *OL Hallenbach* was dragged in by *Olympic's* huge

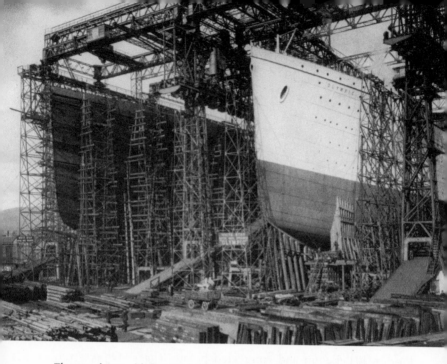

The two sisters, side by side, in the specially constructed Arrol Gantry, in Harland & Wolff shipyard, Belfast.

propeller and consequently needed repairs to its stern and rudder. On this occasion, there was no damage to *Titanic's* older sister unlike a few months later, when leaving Southampton, on her fifth voyage to New York, the Royal Navy Cruiser HMS *Hawke* smashed into *Olympic's* starboard side, shattering its own bow and almost capsizing with the impact, while leaving *Olympic* with two deep gashes above and below the waterline. The voyage was cancelled but there were no fatalities. Little did stewardess Violet Jessop and stoker Arthur John Priest realise that they had personally embarked on the first of a trilogy of disasters concerning the three White Star sister ships. *Olympic* was patched up to enable

The Hole in the "Olympic," the Damage Below the Waterline being Much Greater Than That Above

The Bow of the "Hawke," the Damage being so Great That the Ram Has Been Mashed Flat

A battered-looking HMS *Hawke*, following her infamous 1911 collision with RMS *Olympic*.

a return to Belfast for a more thorough repair job that delayed *Titanic*'s completion. Meanwhile, the crash proved costly to White Star Line as the ensuing inquiry laid the blame entirely on *Olympic* with the Royal Navy claiming that she had pulled the *Hawke* into her.

Following six weeks of repair, *Olympic* was back at work by 30 November 1911 until three months later, on returning to Southampton from New York, she hit something in the ocean that cost her a blade from her propeller. *Titanic* workers in Belfast repaired her once more, and this was the last time that the two sisters were together.

When Captain Smith left *Olympic* for *Titanic*, he was replaced by the unfortunately named Captain Herbert James Haddock. A few months later *Olympic*'s wireless operator, Ernest James Moore, received a distress call from *Titanic* who was over 500 miles away. Captain Haddock had the engines set at full power and raced to her assistance. Four hundred miles later he received a message from Arthur Rostron, the captain of the RMS *Carpathia*: 'All boats accounted for. About 675 souls saved. *Titanic* foundered at 2.20am.' In other words, *Olympic* might as well turn back, but Captain Haddock wanted to help in some way and offered to take the survivors back to England. Captain Rostron flatly refused his offer out of consideration for the effect that *Titanic*'s mirror image might have on her stressed and grieving survivors. There was nothing for it but to return to Southampton after cancelling all entertainments to mark the tragic loss of life.

However, *Olympic* had much to contribute in the aftermath of the sinking; she was used in both the British and American investigations and was examined to see how fast she could turn to determine at what point *Titanic* should have been able to avoid the iceberg.

One inevitable result of the sinking was that an extra 44 lifeboats were added to the 20 on *Olympic*. That was the good news. The bad news was that the extra boats were second-hand collapsible boats, some of which were rotten and could not open. Understandably, the crew baulked at this and just before she set sail, at the end of April 1912, 284 firemen went on strike, demanding that the collapsibles be replaced by wooden boats, despite the fact they had been judged seaworthy by an inspector from the Board of Trade. Meanwhile 100 non-union members were brought on board to cover for the strikers.

On 25 April, four collapsibles were tested in front of the strikers and only one was found to be unseaworthy. It was hoped that the firemen would be appeased by a fresh replacement but now they wanted the non-union workers removed from *Olympic*. When White Star Line rejected this, 54 sailors disembarked, effectively throwing the sailing schedule into disarray. On shore, the sailors were arrested and charged with mutiny, the judge found them guilty but declined to punish them, no doubt due to the recent tragedy. Fearing a public outcry, White Star Line allowed the men to rejoin *Olympic*. In October, the ship returned to Harland & Wolff to be renovated according to the findings of the *Titanic* inquiries, this time without any worn collapsible lifeboats. The newly-improved *Olympic*, with Captain Haddock, was back in action in March 1913.

More changes would be required the following year with the outbreak of war. *Olympic* was painted grey and her port-holes were covered up. Not surprisingly, the number of transatlantic passengers dipped significantly with the threat of enemy U-boats, making *Olympic* too expensive to run, and her final commercial voyage, in October 1914, involved just 153 paying customers. Keeping a nervous eye out for submarines was not the only distraction, as six days into the journey, *Olympic* responded to a distress signal from British warship HMS *Audacious* which had struck a mine off Tory Island in the Atlantic, northwest of the Irish mainland. Two hundred and fifty crew were rescued by *Olympic* while three failed attempts were made to tow *Audacious* to safety before she finally sank. The commander of the Home Fleet, Admiral John Jellicoe, ordered *Olympic* to be held in custody in Lough Swilly as he did not want the British nation to know that one of their warships was lost in case it damaged morale. Although, the morale of *Olympic's* passengers must have been challenged when they found themselves prevented from sending or receiving any messages, or from disembarking the ship, until six days later, on 2 November, when the ship finally sailed on to Belfast.

In May 1915, *Olympic* was requisitioned by the Admiralty as a troop transport while her sister, *Britannic*, who was still under construction, was requisitioned as a hospital ship. *Olympic*, armed with 12 pounders and 4.7 inch guns, could carry up to 6,000 soldiers and would probably outrun any U-boat. In 1916, she was chartered by the Canadian government and became a great favourite with the Canadians as she ferried thousands of them on their way to battle and then brought them safely home again. They even named a dance hall after her, the Olympic Gardens, in Halifax, Nova Scotia.

The following year, the Americans entered the war and *Olympic* found herself ferrying US troops to Britain. On the morning of 12 May 1918, her crew spotted a surfaced U-boat 500 metres straight ahead and, with guns blazing, *Olympic* rammed it. The propeller that had previously caused her so much trouble was now her saving grace as it sliced through the hull of the submarine, which was abandoned by its German crew. Ignoring the survivors in the water, *Olympic* continued to Cherbourg. This seems a callous act today, but it would have been too risky to delay in case there was a second submarine in the area. Later, this achievement was commemorated in a plaque that was paid for by her American passengers.

She left an impressive war record, ferrying over 200,000 soldiers while clocking up 184,000 miles, earning herself the nickname 'Old Reliable'. After the war, she, like thousands and thousands of soldiers, removed her uniform and returned to civilian life and, because of her likeness to *Titanic*, she became very popular with the big stars of the 1920s' cinema, including Charlie Chaplin and Cary Grant. In fact, Chaplin refers to the ship a couple of times in his 1964 autobiography. He knew he had made it big when he could afford to travel first class on *Olympic*. For his previous trip state-side, he had to settle for one of her second-class cabins but enjoyed a brief tour by a steward who showed him the first-class luxury suites.

After sailing on *Olympic*, Max Perkins was a changed man. Editor for the likes of F Scott Fitzgerald and Ernest Hemingway, Perkins was not a natural traveller. Initially unhappy on board, he complained about the lengthy meals and felt imprisoned, albeit in luxury. At some point, however, he fell in love with his surround-ings and joked about running away to sea.

There were still more crashes to come. On 22 March 1924, while reversing out of New York's harbour, *Olympic*'s stern collided with a smaller liner, the *Fort St George*, leaving the smaller ship in need of extensive repairs. A more serious collision occurred ten years later when, approaching New York in a heavy fog, *Olympic* tore through the lightship, *Nantucket Lightship LV-117*, cutting her into two and sinking her. Seven men died, obliging a full investigation into the incident.

Olympic left New York for Britain for the last time on 5 April 1935. Following a career involving 257 round trips, 480,000 passengers and approximately 4 collisions, it was time to retire. A few months later she was sold to Sir John Jarvis for £97,500 and was finally demolished in 1937. Such a pity she was not kept in one piece as an homage to her two sisters and her own success.

HMHS *BRITANNIC*, (HIS MAJESTY'S HOSPITAL SHIP)
(1911–1916)

Titanic's doomed little sister, who would not make a seventh voyage.

Britannic's keel was laid on 30 November 1911. Initially called *Gigantic*, she was re-christened following the *Titanic* tragedy with several new modifications, including an increase in the number of lifeboats she would carry. Forty-eight lifeboats were on board, 46 of which were the biggest lifeboats ever placed on a ship. She was 852 feet long and weighed 50,000 tonnes, making her longer and heavier than *Olympic,* and was launched on 26 February 1914. White Star Line's financial problems delayed her completion and she eventually made her maiden voyage, to Moudras, Greece, on 23 December 1915. The First World War had broken out and she had been requisitioned by the British government as a hospital ship.

On 12 November 1916, *Britannic* left Southampton for her sixth voyage, heading to Moudras. She was carrying 1,065 people: 673 crew, 77 nurses and 315 RAMC (Royal Army Medical Corps). By 21 November, she was sailing at full speed (21 knots) between the islands of Makronissos and Kea. It was after eight o'clock in the morning and those on board, including stewardess Violet Jessop who had sailed on both *Olympic* and *Titanic*, were enjoying their breakfast.

According to Violet, a sudden explosion caused the ship to 'shiver'. Many thought they had hit a smaller boat. Ten minutes later, due to damaged watertight doors, *Britannic* was already list-ing to the side and was in as much trouble as her sister had been within an hour after hitting the iceberg. Lots of porthole win-dows were open because the nurses were airing the wards and this resulted in a speedy intake of water.

Kea Island was three miles away and *Britannic*'s Captain Charles Bartlett decided to try beaching her and gave the order to turn

TEN MINUTES LATER, DUE TO DAMAGED WATERTIGHT DOORS, *BRITANNIC* WAS ALREADY LISTING TO THE SIDE

her towards Kea's shoreline. Meanwhile, someone started releasing lifeboats not realising that the ship's propellers were out of the water. An inevitable blood bath ensued. Fortunately, for a third lifeboat, the engines and, thus, propellers were switched off in the nick of time. At 8.35am, Captain Bartlett ordered everyone to abandon ship. Fifteen minutes later, he felt that the flooding had slowed and had the engines switched back on, to make a second attempt to reach Kea. By 9am, however, he accepted that the ship was doomed and sounded out her whistle to indicate 'All hands off the ship', before walking into the sea to swim to the nearest lifeboat. This meant that the engineers could leave as, just like *Titanic's* heroes, they had remained hard at work, trying to keep the ship afloat. *Britannic* made her final plunge at 9.07am. Thirty officers and crew were lost.

In her memoir, *Testament of Youth*, the writer and activist Vera Brittain wrote of her wartime experiences. In November 1916, she was working as a nurse in Malta and remembers a collective shock amongst the British contingent over *Britannic*'s loss. She visited a friend in hospital, a young nurse, who had been on the ship that morning, and found her in a state of distress. The friend described how the nursing staff were quietly marched out of the dining room and told to fetch their valuables. One flustered girl grabbed her fountain pen but left all her money behind. On the boat deck, their elderly matron refused to leave until she had accounted for all her staff, and not one nurse was lost. The women got into the lifeboats while the medical officers shimmied down the ropes and dropped into the sea to swim to the boats, though two of them never surfaced from their fall. Only the matron saw what happened, the propellers lacerating limbs and torsos, sending bodies into the air, but she never said a word. They were in the boats for three hours before being rescued by two destroyers, whose crew were mistakenly searching for *Britannic*, refusing to believe she was gone.

An investigation concluded that the ship had hit a mine, while Captain Bartlett reported there was evidence that she had been hit by two torpedoes.

Her wreck was discovered in 1975 by French oceanographer Jacques Yves Cousteau, 120 metres down and lying on her starboard side. Since then she has been explored several times, including by Doctor Robert Ballard's expedition in 1995.

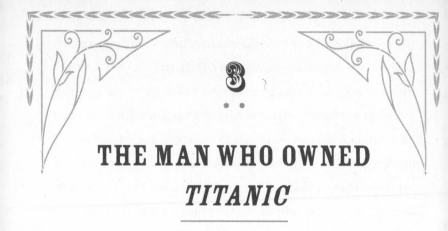

THE MAN WHO OWNED
TITANIC

One of the more ludicrous *Titanic* theories is that the ship was purposely sunk by her owner, the American banker John Pierpoint (JP) Morgan, to rid himself of competitors and opponents. He was holidaying in France, and legend has it that his suite B52, which was meant to have been specially designed for him, was booked and ready for his return journey but the seventy-five-year-old pleaded illness at the last minute and *Titanic* set sail without him. However, there is no evidence to confirm that he was to board *Titanic* for his journey home. Like any self-respecting billionaire, he had his own yacht, the luxurious *Corsair II*, whose 292 feet was a third of *Titanic*'s length and quite capable of crossing the Atlantic. Nevertheless, it is difficult to believe that he would have preferred his 'old' yacht over the new biggest ship in the world. After all, he had travelled to Belfast to see her launched. In any case, his *Titanic* suite was his for whenever he needed it and, in Morgan's absence, it easily accommodated three men, Bruce Ismay, his valet, John Fry, and secretary, William Harrison. Two

JP Morgan did not like having his picture taken. This photograph shows him looking furious as he is seemingly held back from attacking the photographer, or the camera, with his walking stick. This mulish behaviour was down to his self-consciousness over his nose. As a child, he had suffered from a skin condition called rosacea, which, in turn, developed into rhinophyma, leaving him with a misshapen, purple nose and a hatred for publicity, while all his professional photographs had to be re-touched.

days after the tragedy, a newspaper reporter found Mr Morgan at the Grand Hotel in the French health resort of Aix-les-Bains with his French mistress.

By 1901, Morgan was one of the wealthiest people in the world, with a personal fortune worth billions. Physically, he was a big man with large shoulders and a broad chest and this largeness was complemented by a forceful personality. This was a man who advised presidents, ruled Wall Street, founded US steel, organised General Electric, bought out lagging business after business, only to rebuild them into bludgeoning, profitable versions of their former selves, and looked to dominate the business world via the rail track and the oceans. His life, as far as banking and business is concerned, is one long blistering success story.

In fact, America has much to thank him for because his legacy included more than thriving industries. He was a benefactor of such notable institutions as the American Museum of Natural History, the Metropolitan Museum of Art and Harvard University. He was also an avid collector of art, books and gemstones. Indeed, after his death, his art collection was valued at $50 million. He had his own library in New York, cared for by his own librarian, which remains a popular landmark to this day. His massive collection of gemstones won awards at the Trade Fair in Paris. In 1906, he was approached by Edward Curtis, a self-taught photographer, who wanted to document the lives and culture of the American Indians before there was nothing left to record. Curtis needed a generous patron and he set his sights on JP Morgan. He wrote a letter to

HIS LIFE, AS FAR AS BANKING AND BUSINESS IS CONCERNED, IS ONE LONG BLISTERING SUCCESS STORY.

the banker, outlining his ambitious project, to which he received a curt reply, 'Mr Curtis, there are many demands on me for financial assistance. I will be unable to help you.' However, when Curtis sent some of his photographs, Morgan was immediately hooked, complimenting the photographer on his work and telling him that he wanted to see his pictures inside the most beautiful books. He agreed to give Curtis $75,000 over five years in exchange for 500 original prints which became the 20-book series *The North American Indian* – possibly one of the most important works ever published and containing what must surely be some of the most stunning photographs ever taken of the Native Americans.

At some point, it became necessary for White Star Line to write to the port authorities in New York and ask that they expand the harbour for their massive liners. Their request was refused until JP Morgan stepped in and made it so. He had bought the shipping line in 1902, via the International Maritime Marine Company

(IMM), hungry to profit from the rising demand for transatlantic travel, and told Bruce Ismay, chairman of White Star, to get him the 'finest vessels afloat'.

The banker was in Belfast to see *Titanic* launched on 31 May 1911. As one of the more distinguished guests, he dined in Harland & Wolff's boardroom at Queen's Island before stepping onto the *Nomadic* to be ferried out for a brief tour of the *Olympic*, who was due to make her maiden voyage.

One can only guess at Morgan's reaction to the tragic news of *Titanic*'s sinking. In a newspaper article in the *Daily Sketch*, dated 23 April 1912, Philip Franklin, the American vice-president of IMMC, is quoted as saying that he was with the two directors, Mr Morgan and Mr Steele, when the sinking was confirmed. This is incorrect. In the official transcripts of the American Senate's 1912 investigation, Franklin says he telephoned the two directors with the awful news. Later, Morgan said that 'Monetary losses amount to nothing in life. It is the loss of life that counts. It is that frightful death.'

He apparently suffered enormous guilt over the deaths of over 1,500 passengers and crew on a ship he had commissioned. He died in his sleep eleven months later, on 31 March 1913, in Rome. The New York stock markets shut down for two hours while his body was brought through the city on its journey to Cedar Hill Cemetery in Hartford, Connecticut, his birthplace.

4

WINGED AND FOUR-LEGGED PASSENGERS

There were maybe twelve dogs on *Titanic* of which two or three would survive. Only those travelling in first class could bring their dogs with them. *Titanic* had excellent kennel facilities on the F deck. These first-class dogs were the responsibility of John Hutchinson, the ship's carpenter, and were exercised daily on the poop deck by either a steward or a bellboy, and a dog show had been planned for the morning of 15 April. Not everyone, however, appreciated the sight of doting owners with their pets. In a letter to a friend, the American painter Francis Davis Millet complained about the *'obnoxious, ostentatious American women'* with their *'tiny dogs ... leading husbands around like pet lambs'*.

A few of the dogs belonged to some of the wealthiest people in the world. The millionaire John Jacob Astor brought his Airdale, Kitty, with him. Clothing manufacturer Martin Rothschild and his wife had their Pekingese. Publisher Henry Sleeper Harper had his prize Pekingese, Sun Yat-sen, while a banker from Philadelphia, Robert W Daniel, had bought a prize-winning French bulldog in

Britain and was bringing it home to America. Harry Anderson had his Chow-Chow dog, while William Carter had his elderly Airdale and a King Charles Spaniel, for whom he later claimed $200 from the White Star Line.

Fifty pairs of English foxhounds had a lucky escape when their new owner Clarence Moore, from Washington, booked them passage on another ship, while he himself boarded *Titanic*. Moore, a well-known banker and horseman, went down with the ship, having refused several times to get into a lifeboat.

Another fortunate dog was Captain Smith's Russian wolfhound, Ben, who spent one night on *Titanic* before being sent home to the captain's daughter.

Margaret Hays was accompanied by two girlfriends and Lady, her Pomeranian. That night, Hays wrapped Lady in blankets and the three girls made their way to the lifeboats, getting into Lifeboat 7. In the boat were two scared unaccompanied little boys, who could only speak French. Fluent in French, Margaret took it upon herself to mind them and they played with Lady until they were rescued by *Carpathia*. Margaret brought the boys – four-year-old Michel and two-year-old Edmond – back to New York to care for them until somebody claimed them. It transpired that the boys' father had snatched them from his estranged wife in France. Mr Navratil went down with *Titanic*, while their frantic mother happened to see their photograph in a newspaper

Four-year-old Michel and his baby brother were travelling under false names their father had given them, Lola and Momon.

and sailed to America to retrieve them.

A woman who had been named as American Ann Elizabeth Isham (1862–1912) was very attached to her Great Dane, whom she visited every day on *Titanic*. When he was prevented from getting into a lifeboat, she chose to stay with him. Two days after the sinking, when ships went out searching for bodies, she was found, her arms wrapped around her pet, the two of them frozen together. It would appear, in recent years, that there is no evidence to support this woman as being the owner of the Great Dane, so it remains a mystery to this day – both the identity of this female passenger and why Ann Elizabeth Isham, a first-class female passenger, did not end up in a lifeboat. A story appeared in the *Daily*

Sketch on 6 May 1912 about a young woman who refused to leave her dog, a Saint Bernard, who was, according to the paper, a great favourite on board. Her body was later found floating alongside her pet. Furthermore, Mrs Johanna Stunke, a passenger on the German ship SS *Bremen* that passed through the area where *Titanic* sank, told of seeing over a hundred bodies in the ocean, including that of a woman who appeared to embrace a large, shaggy dog that Mrs Stunke thought might be a Saint Bernard. However, it is possible that the woman in the water could have been wearing a fur coat which, at a glance, might have imitated the appearance of the dog, giving the impression of a 'shaggy' coat.

Helen Bishop (1892–1916) survived the sinking but felt it would be frowned upon if she brought her new dog, Frou-Frou, a Toy Poodle into a lifeboat with so many people needing saving. She found it difficult to leave him behind, in her cabin, as he was clearly scared, biting hold of her dress and refusing to let go.

The only dogs to survive were the Pekingese and the two Pomeranians as their small size meant they could be easily hidden in the lifeboats.

At some point, the passengers on *Titanic's* deck were joined by the rest of the dogs. Someone, who was rumoured to be John Jacob Astor, had opened their kennels and one can imagine their excitement at being freed to roam the ship together. Doubtless too, they would have quickly picked up on, and then shared, the passengers' fear and anxiety.

Jenny was the resident cat. Just like some of her fellow crew, she

THERE WERE ALSO FOUR FRENCH ROOSTERS AND HENS ON BOARD, COURTESY OF FIRST-CLASS PASSENGER ELLA HOLMES WHITE.

transferred from *Olympic* to take her up position as *Titanic's* mascot and official exterminator of rats and mice. According to stewardess Violet Jessop, Jenny was fed by the kitchen staff and took a fancy to a scullion called Jim – though Violet was known to use different names for people so Jim might well have been called something else. In any case, Jenny had four kittens in the week before *Titanic* left Southampton for Cherbourg and then there are two possible endings for what happened next. The first is that they all went down with the ship or else – and this is a much more attractive ending – legend has it that, at Southampton, Jenny had a quick look around before deciding to remove her kittens, one by one, off *Titanic*. Are cats psychic or is it a case of cats needing to move their newborns shortly after birth? A story is told about a stoker who got a job on *Titanic* and was being urged by his mate to travel to New York. In two minds whether to stay on *Titanic* or look for another job, his decision to leave was made after seeing Jenny take her family off the ship.

There were also four French roosters and hens on board, courtesy of first-class passenger Ella Holmes White. She was bringing them back to New York to improve her poultry stock. Presumably they shared F deck with the dogs.

Second-class passenger Elizabeth Nye was travelling with her yellow canary, while another woman was thought to have brought thirty cockerels with her. A very fortunate canary is the one that disembarked at Cherbourg. Mr Meanwell, who had moved to France, had had the bird put on *Titanic*, where it resided in the office of Chief Purser Hugh McElroy.

And what of the rats and mice? One might imagine that there could not have been too many on a maiden voyage, but what about the couple of years that *Titanic* spent under construction at the shipyard when crusts from workers' lunches could have attracted a silent following. Masseuse Maude Slocombe had to bin a half-eaten mouldy sandwich from the Turkish bath before she could open it up to passengers. One rat made its presence known when it ran across the floor of the third-class dining room, causing several women to burst into tears. This supposedly took place on Sunday evening, 14 April 1912.

5

LOST TREASURES

DIAMONDS

One might meet with varying opinions as to what is defined by the word 'treasure'. A small article appeared in the *Daily Sketch* newspaper on Thursday, 18 April 1912, about diamonds and furs on *Titanic*. According to the article, there were several diamond merchants on board, whose fate had not yet been determined, and they had with them a large quantity of insured stock.

Over the years, this story has caused a lot of speculation, with a newer version emerging that the diamond merchants were two Swiss brothers, although no such men are listed amongst the passengers. In 2000, a fruitless search of the wreck was made to salvage what was believed to be £200 million worth of diamonds.

In fact, there was *one* diamond merchant on board, twenty-five-year old Jakob Birbaum, from Antwerp, Belgium, who worked in San Francisco as his family's sales representative. He had returned home to restock, extending his visit to include the Jewish holiday Passover and, then, wishing to return to San Francisco as soon as possible, he booked himself a first-class ticket on *Titanic*. Family lore has his relatives pleading with him against boarding a ship on its maiden voyage, but he assured everyone that the ship was 'practically unsinkable'. His body was recovered by the *Mackay-Bennett* and sent back to Belgium, in May, via New York, and was buried in the Jewish Cemetery, in Putte, Holland.

ORCHIDS

A fantastic article appeared in the Sunday edition of the *San Francisco Call* newspaper on 28 April 1912, about the 500 Indian orchids that were on their way to California. They were, according to the paper, *Vanda Coerulea* orchids, rare to that side of the world, and American growers were excited about introducing them to the Pacific coast. A cutting of the article was sent to the British *Daily Sketch* newspaper from an Irish reader in California, and the paper took the opportunity to boast about having a Californian-based fan – that is, the sender of the article – while mentioning the *Titanic* orchid consignment. Quite wisely, no reference is made to the *Call*'s sensational account about the bodies of victims lying in the Atlantic, adorned with the precious orchids. The journalist – and that term is used rather gingerly – chooses a man, two women (a peasant and a lady) and a young child to present an all-encompassing sentimental scene for the readers. The better dressed woman is specifically named as 'a woman of fashion' who was used to wearing orchids on the belt of her dresses and now lay in the water, a bunch of the rare orchids caught at her waist. The child was dead on the 'crest of a wave' with an orchid in its 'chubby hand.' And so forth, although there is no mention of the *Vanda Coerulea*'s most striking aspect, they are one of the few orchids with blue flowers.

In an unfortunate choice of accompanying material, page 32 of the same edition is entirely dedicated to San Francisco's Free Public School of Navigation, with the heading, 'Do You Want To Be Captain Of An Ocean Liner?'

JOSEPH CONRAD MANUSCRIPT & LADY AUGUSTA GREGORY'S GIFT

Irish playwright and poet Lady Gregory sent her American-based lover, art-collector John Quinn, a ring which, to his apparent relief, went down on *Titanic*.

Irish American John Quinn was not on the *Titanic*. Born on 14 April in 1870, in Ohio, the ambitious Quinn worked and studied hard, becoming a successful lawyer in New York and getting involved in politics. He swapped careers in 1912, after tiring of New York politics, and set himself up as a major collector and patron of the arts. His new vocation was varied and of lasting importance, from defending James Joyce's novel *Ulysses* in court against charges of obscenity, a case he lost (at some point he admitted to the judge that he didn't understand the novel himself and felt that perhaps Joyce had gone too far with his method), to becoming one of the first Americans to buy and champion modern European art. Polish British writer Joseph Conrad had plenty of reason to be grateful to Quinn, who bought most of the handwritten manuscripts of the writer's short stories and novels. Quinn's most recent purchase in 1912 was Conrad's short story 'Karain'. The writer had posted it out to him, but it never reached New York, and both men guessed it must have been on *Titanic*.

The collector had many famous friends, some of the finest artists and writers of the day, like James Joyce, Ezra Pound, TS Elliot, WB Yeats, Maud Gonne, Sir Roger Casement and Douglas Hyde. He had love affairs with quite a few women, including Irish playwright, poet and co-founder of Dublin's Abbey Theatre, Lady Augusta Gregory, who, at sixty years of age, spent some time with him in New York. Back home in Ireland, in 1912, she posted off several love letters but failed to receive equally ardent replies. She sent him a gift, a ring that was sitting in the Mail Room on *Titanic*.

When it was lost, Lady Gregory described it as a 'gloomy omen', signifying that the romantic relationship was lost too. Quinn mentioned the ring in a letter to the painter Augustus John, wondering if he wasn't better off without it. However, his attitude was kinder in a letter to her when he described the loss of the ring along with his Conrad manuscript as being real and personal. It might have been kinder still to forgo mentioning the manuscript and leave it at just missing the ring, but perhaps he was mindful of not toying with her emotions.

RUBÁIYÁT OF OMAR KHAYYÁM

Omar Khayyám (1048–1131) was a Persian poet, mathematician and astronomer. Edward Fitzgerald (1809–1883) was an English poet and writer who, thanks to his parents' wealth, led an enviable life of ease. He was briefly and unhappily married to the daughter of a fellow poet, but it appears that his true gift was for friendship with the likes of William Makepeace Thackery, Lord Alfred Tennyson and Thomas Carlyle – the cream of the Victorian literary world. In the 1850s, he became interested in first Spanish and then Persian poetry, befriending Edward Cowell – perhaps the only Victorian to speak Persian – and it is then that his pen crossed with Omar Khayyám's, whose literary legacy included a series of stanzas about wine, good times and the inevitable passing of time. Fitzgerald translated the work into English and, in 1859, published it as the *Rubáiyát of Omar Khayyám*. Jump forward fifty years to 1909 when

Sangorski and Sutcliffe, the British bookbinding firm, was commissioned by Sotheran's Bookshop, in London, to rebind an edition of Fitzgerald's *Rubáiyát*. This would be no ordinary edition. Francis Sangorski spent two months designing the book which would take him two years to complete and involved 1,500 emeralds, rubies, amethysts and topazes, amongst others, with 5,000 pieces of inlaid Turkish and Moroccan leather and 600 sheets of 22-carat gold leaf. The cover was adorned with three peacocks, symbols of Persia and, for all we know, the book and *Titanic* were created simultaneously, letter by letter, rivet by rivet. When it was finished in 1911, it was priced at £1000 and sent to New York to be put on display. However, Sotheran's refused to pay the big bill, set by customs, and the book was returned to them. They sent it for auction at Sotheby's where, on 29 March 1912, due to a coal strike, it sold for a mere £450, ironically, to an American buyer. Against the wishes of a lot of British people who felt that that such a beautiful piece should remain in the country, it ended up on *Titanic* on its way to the new owner.

After the book was lost, in April 1912, Sangorski decided to recreate it but drowned trying to save a woman's life, six weeks later. His partner, Stanley Bray, was determined to carry on with the project and spent the next six years making a second book using Francis's notes. Unfortunately, that edition was lost during the Blitz in the Second World War, despite the fact that it was inside a safe in the vault of a bank. Undaunted, Bray embarked on yet another edition, which his wife donated to the British Library after he died.

La Circassienne au bain.

The woman who cost White Star
Line a small fortune.

LA CIRCASSIENNE AU BAIN

When the painting *La Circassienne au Bain* first went on display in
the Louvre, in 1814, the critics were far from impressed. Merry-
Joseph Blondel (1781–1853) was the painter and most critics preferred his earlier work to this neoclassical life-sized portrait of
a young Circassian woman performing her morning ablutions.
While her beauty could not be denied, she was criticised for the
awkward turning of her body that many felt lacked grace. Over
the next eleven years, however, as Blondel's reputation improved,
so did opinions about the portrait, which proved popular in
printed reproductions.

In 1912, the painting was the property of Håkan Mauritz
Björnström-Steffanson, a young Swede, who was on his way to
Washington. He receives three mentions in Walter Lord's book,

A Night to Remember, making it impossible to forget that he was drinking a hot lemonade in the first-class smoking room just before – and after – *Titanic* hit the iceberg, and we may assume that it was that same hot lemonade he was sipping when a ship's officer appeared, advising the late-night drinkers and gamblers to fetch their life jackets. Björnström-Steffanson, along with first-class passenger Hugh Woolner, had a busy night ahead. It is they who helped Mrs Helen Churchill Candee into Lifeboat 6. Then, later, when it became necessary to guard the remaining lifeboats against hordes of desperate men, it is Björnström-Steffanson and Woolner who helped to forcibly remove male bodies from Collapsible C. When their work was done on A Deck, they made for the Promenade Deck and were obliged to climb the railings to escape the lapping of the ocean. They spotted Collapsible D being lowered down the side of *Titanic* and, seeing that there was plenty of room, flung themselves in its direction, crash-landing into it. Thanks to their quick thinking, they both survived. In the posthumous memoir, *The Way It Was: Walter Lord on His Life and Books,* a collection of his writings and interviews as edited by his friend Jenny Lawrence, Lord says that Björnström-Steffanson, who became a prosperous New York banker, refused to be interviewed for *A Night to Remember* and that he feels that the Swede may have been embarrassed about getting into a lifeboat.

On reaching New York, several of the well-heeled survivors, including Björnström-Steffanson, formed a committee to honour *Carpathia*'s Captain Arthur Rostron and his crew for their bravery.

Today, the Swede is remembered for something other than surviving the sinking. In January 1913, he submitted a compensation claim to White Star Line for his Blondel painting, *La Circassienne au Bain*, for $100,000 (over $2 million in today's money) which was by far the biggest single claim made by a White Star passenger.

On 16 January 1913, *The New York Times* published an article on the claims made by *Titanic* survivors and it makes for somewhat peculiar reading. The journalist picks out the Blondel painting and pitches it against the claim made by Mary McGovern who wished to be compensated $50 for the loss of two crochet collars that had been sent from Ireland by her mother. Meanwhile, the wealthy Mrs Charlotte Cardeza, who listed out the items of her lost 14 cases included, on top of the cost of her drowned diamond jewellery and fancy ballgowns, $1.75 for a bar of soap.

ARTISTS AND WRITERS

HELEN CHURCHILL CANDEE (NÉE HUNGERFORD)
(1859–1949)

F ifty-two-year old divorcee Helen Churchill Candee was possibly ahead of her time. Years earlier, she had divorced an alcoholic husband and supported herself and two children by writing magazine articles and a popular novel, in which some of her Oklahoma neighbours recognised themselves amongst her cast of characters. In the early 1900s, she went to Washington DC and set herself up as an interior decorator, an unusual move at the time. She must have been first rate, however, as her clients soon included President Theodore Roosevelt amongst others, while her social life encompassed the world of the arts, politics and the burgeoning suffragette movement. She was in Paris, in April 1912, researching for a book, when she received word that her son had been in an accident. She booked herself onto the first ship available to return to America as fast as she could. On *Titanic*, she spent much of her time with painter Francis Davis Millet, Colonel Archibald Gracie and American President William Howard Taft's

Helen Churchill Candee is believed to be the woman directly behind the parade's leader, Mrs RC Burleson. A hundred women needed hospital treatment by the time they finished marching in the 1913 suffragette parade in Washington DC.

military aide Major Archibald Butt. President Taft and his wife were also clients of her interior-decorating business. This was the sort of company she was used to, and one may assume that she made a worthy companion thanks to her two professions and elite social standing. Certainly, Walter Lord mentions that quite a few of the first-class men wanted to take care of her. Hugh Woolner and Håkan Björnström-Steffanson escorted her to Lifeboat 6, although, on her way into the boat, she broke her ankle in a fall. A few newspapers circulated the story that she had broken both her legs, but this was an exaggeration. Nevertheless, despite her pain, she and fellow passenger Margaret Brown helped with the rowing. Churchill wrote an account of what happened that night for *Collier's Weekly*, a popular magazine, and you can read 'Sealed Orders' at www.encyclopedia-titanic.org. Some feel that she alludes to a special gentleman on *Titanic*, who could have been Hugh Woolner or New York architect Edward Austin Kent. Walter Lord believed it was to Kent that she handed an ivory cameo of her mother, along with a small bottle of brandy, for safekeeping. The items were later retrieved from Kent's body and in 2006 sold at an auction, the cameo for approximately $80,000 and the bottle for $40,000.

Helen Churchill Candee did not make a habit of talking about *Titanic* out of respect for those who had lost their lives and neither did she waste the rest of hers. One might be reminded of the character of Rose, as played by Kate Winslet in James Cameron's film *Titanic*, when having been spared after watching Jack, her true love die, she feels bound to live life to the full. In 1913, the day before the presidential inauguration of Woodrow Wilson, Mrs Churchill Candee was one of the riders at the head of a 'Votes for Women' parade. During the First World War, she joined the Royal Italian Red Cross and one of her patients, in Milan, was the American writer Ernest Hemingway. After the war, she embarked on yet another career, that of fearless explorer in the likes of China, Japan, Indonesia and Cambodia, trekking through jungles on the back of an elephant, after which she wrote two books about her experiences that saw her honoured by the French government, the King of Cambodia and King George V. She gave lectures and wrote countless articles about her exotic destinations and then, in 1935, she became one of the founding members of the Society of Woman Geographers. In her later years, she started writing for *National Geographic* magazine. She died in August 1949, a couple of months shy of her ninetieth birthday.

JACQUES HEATH FUTRELLE (1875–1912)

After the sinking, Jacques Heath Futrelle's widow wished that her husband had become drunk at his birthday party because if he did then surely they would have missed boarding *Titanic* in Southampton. However, that would have been completely out of character. As it was, they cut it rather fine and had to rush to get there on time. The thirty-seven-year-old was possibly the most commercially successful writer on the ship. In 1895, he married writer Lily May Peel and they moved to New York where he began

Jacques Heath Futrelle.

writing for the *New York Herald*. The literary couple enjoyed their new social life, befriending other writers such as Edith Wharton and O Henry and then they moved again, this time to Boston, where he wrote for the daily tabloid paper the *Boston American*. His most popular creation first appeared in 1905, The Thinking Machine, or Professor Augustus S.F.X.Van Dusen, who could solve impossible crimes with his superior brain. Some believe that the crime writer Agatha Christie was inspired by the brainy sleuth who went on to appear in over 40 stories and novels. In 1912, Mr and Mrs Futrelle had travelled to Europe to sign foreign contracts for his books, and he continued writing on board *Titanic*. Sailing on the biggest ship in the world must have been a thrill for Futrelle who had a real interest in technology. Thanks to Father Browne, Futrelle is captured forevermore, standing on the boat deck outside the gymnasium. The writer had mistaken the Isle of Wight for France and asked the priest why the English did not cross there when the shores were so close to one another. Father Browne described Futrelle's voice as loud and penetrating but suspected he was being addressed by someone of importance based on his expensive-looking clothes.

His wife described how he died a true hero. Mrs Futrelle had her own grief to contend with, but it must have been compounded by the fact that at least one newspaper had listed Jacques amongst the living. Therefore, she had the unenviable task of breaking the sad news to her daughter and sister-in-law, who were overjoyed that both husband and wife had survived. Three times she tried to get Jacques into her lifeboat and three times he removed her arms from him, finally finding it necessary to scream at her to go, for God's sake. Just go. How he must have longed to do as she bid but would not, could not, save himself. Eventually a ship's officer forced her into the lifeboat. As the ship sank, she thought she could see him on the deck waving at her. His body was never found. Three months later his mother died, the family believing her heart had been broken by Jacques's death. Two novels were published posthumously, one of them, *My Lady's Garter*, was inscribed by Mrs Futrelle: 'To the heroes of *Titanic*, I dedicate my husband's book'.

FRANCIS DAVIS MILLET (1846–1912)

First-class passenger, Francis Davis Millet, an American, did not survive the sinking. Millet, a painter, was sixty-five years old in April 1912, and one cannot but be inspired by the lengthy list of his achievements, which begins with his accompanying his surgeon father to the American Civil War, initially as drummer boy to a Massachusetts regiment, before becoming a surgeon's assistant. Next, he graduated from Harvard with a Master of Arts degree and became a reporter and then editor of the *Boston Courier*. After that, he decided to devote himself to art and enrolled at the Royal Academy of Fine Arts in Antwerp, winning medals for his work. At some point, he learned to speak either five or six languages. When war broke out between Russia and Turkey, in 1877, he turned war correspondent for several American and English newspapers and

Painter Francis Davis Millet,
a man of many talents and
varied interests.

Right: Frontispiece of one of
Millet's works.

was decorated by Russia and Rumania for bravery under fire and his services to the wounded.

Over the next few years he joined various committees for the National Gallery of Art and the Metropolitan Museum of Art, to name but a few. He helped to found the School of the Museum of Fine Arts in Boston and became heavily involved with lots of world's fairs, including the World's Columbian Exposition in Chicago. In 1898, he became a war correspondent again, this time for the Philippine-American war. Meanwhile, he translated the Russian writer Tolstoy into English, and his literary output of articles, short stories and books got him elected to the American Academy of Arts. He was also made an honorary member of the American Institute of Architects. He became a renowned designer and sculptor, designing the Civil War medal in 1907, at the request of the US army and war department. He was appointed head of the American Academy in Rome and his friends included writer Mark Twain and artist John Singer Sargent. Millet was last seen on *Titanic* helping women and children into lifeboats. His body was recovered by the *Mackay-Bennet* and buried in East Bridgewater Central Cemetery, Massachusetts.

EDITH ROSENBAUM
(ALSO KNOWN AS EDITH RUSSELL) (1879–1975)

In her later years, Edith Russell joked about the number of calamities that she had faced in her life, from shipwrecks to fires, car

Producer of a film based on William Lord's *Titanic* book William MacQuitty with Edith Russell and her famous mascot, a wind-up musical pig, given to her by her mother.

crashes to flooding. The only disasters that she had not experienced were the bubonic plague and a husband. In 1911, she narrowly escaped death in Paris, where she was the resident buyer for several New York fashion houses. She was in a car with her fiancé, Ludwig Lowe, and a friend of theirs, that was being driven much too fast by Lowe, who lost control of the vehicle as he took a corner. The car flipped over, smashing into trees, and Edith was the only survivor. After the accident, her mother bought her a musical pig because she heard that the pig was a good luck symbol in France. The toy provided a welcome distraction for the children in Edith's lifeboat on 15 April 1912.

In 1912 Edith was working in France as the first Paris correspondent for the journal *Women's Wear Daily*, launched in 1910, and she would go on to become a leading journalist in the fashion world and spokesperson for *Chambre Syndicale de la Haute Couture Parisienne* (the governing body of the French fashion industry). She also helped style various singers and actresses and established her own clothing line, 'Elrose', for Lord & Taylor department store in New York.

In April 1912, she booked her return ticket to New York on another ship, due to sail on 7 April, but was asked, by her editor, to cover the Easter races in Paris and this delayed her journey until 10 April, whereby she boarded the *Titanic* at Cherbourg. Her luggage was precious, all nineteen pieces of it, filled with Parisian clothes that were destined for her New York clients. The only daughter of wealthy parents, she was clearly making a decent wage too, which allowed her to book a first-class cabin for herself, along with a separate room for her luggage. She had asked about insuring her property but was told it was unnecessary as the ship was unsinkable. At Queenstown, she wrote to her secretary back in Paris, describing *Titanic* as wonderful, while also criticising its lack of cosiness and lamenting the stiff, formal behaviour of its crew. She ended the letter by promising to relax on the trip but could not shake off a feeling that something bad was going to happen. She was undressing at 11.40pm, on 14 April, when she felt the ship shudder, followed by two more jolts necessitating her to hold onto her bed post and then she saw the iceberg from her starboard window. After ensuring that her cases were locked, she spent some time in the first-class lounge, people-watching, until she spied Robert Wareham, her room steward. She gave him the keys to her luggage because, for whatever reason, she believed that *Titanic* was to be towed to Halifax and, therefore, was entrusting her possessions into his temporary care. Taking the key, he warned her that she would not see the luggage again. However, he went to her cabin to retrieve her lucky mascot, the pig her mother had given her, taking care to wrap it in a blanket. Leaving Wareham, she headed for the boat deck, where Bruce Ismay, who knew her, was shocked to find her still on deck and threw her down the steps towards Lifeboat 11. She credited him with saving her life. Two sailors picked her up, but she baulked at the distance between the railing and the suspended lifeboat, insisting that they put her down, which they did. She could not believe that *Titanic* was actually sinking and, apart from everything else, felt her fashionably tight skirt would not allow her to climb the rails. In the end, the decision was made for her when a crewman, thinking the toy in her arms was a baby, grabbed it and threw it into the boat, obliging her to follow it; surely this anonymous crewman was most responsible for saving her. On board *Carpathia*, first-class passenger Henry Stengel remembered her chatting and befriending lots of people.

Not surprisingly, after the sinking, she placed a huge claim over her lost luggage with White Star Line. Robert Wareham, did not survive the sinking but his body was found and buried in Fairview Lawn Cemetery, Halifax, Nova Scotia. No keys were found on him.

During the war, Edith took a break from the world of fashion, exchanging it for three months in the trenches, working as a war correspondent for the American Red Cross. Unfortunately, most of her war articles and letters were never published in full. In 1916, still working in fashion, she initiated a second career, becoming an expert in, and breeding, champion Pekingese dogs. She travelled to shows all over America with her own award-winning dogs.

She appeared in the New York *Sun* newspaper on 1 January 1918, when she was charged with smuggling into America four dresses that were worth over $1000. According to the article, she claimed that she was a non-resident of Paris and the dresses were hers. Three months later she was acquitted by a jury.

In 1920, due to widespread discrimination and hatred for all things German within the post-war French fashion industry, Edith thought it prudent to change her name from Rosenbaum to Russell. Over the next five years, she received service awards both for her fashion and war work. She extended her repertoire, writing for English and Italian fashion magazines as well as giving lectures and keeping up a strenuous travel schedule, with homes on both sides of the Atlantic. Her social life included the likes of Italian leader Benito Mussolini as well as French actor Maurice Chevalier and British actor Peter Lawford's parents. By the mid-1940s, she made Claridge's Hotel, in London, her permanent home, returning briefly to America for the New York premier of the 1953 film, *Titanic*. Back in London, she was one of several advisors on the set of the 1958 film, *A Night to Remember*, which portrays her with her toy pig. She moved, for the last time, to the Embassy House Hotel in London. She could not find a publisher interested in her *Titanic* experience, but she did join the survivors' circuit and was interviewed many times about the sinking, always bringing the pig along. This culminated in her being named an honorary member of the Titanic Historical Society in 1963. By the time Edith died, the pig had stopped making music and Edith probably believed it would never work again, yet, over forty years after her death, its new owners at London's National Maritime Museum got it going once more and a minute-long recording is available on YouTube. It is both fascinating and eerie to hear the tinkling that helped distract the survivors in Lifeboat 11. Following years of debate, the tune was finally identified in 2013 as 'La Sorella', a march composed by Charles Borel-Clerq in 1905.

'Ruthless journalist' William Stead, as described by Lord Alfred Milner. Stead believed himself to be on the 'side of the angels'.

WILLIAM THOMAS STEAD, WHO WAS DROWNED FROM THE "TITANIC," APRIL 14, 1912

WILLIAM STEAD (1849–1912)

On 3 May 1912, the *Daily Sketch* published a moving tribute by Earl Grey to his friend William Stead, whom he called the 'first of journalists'. Earlier, on 26 April, a packed out memorial service had been held in Westminster Chapel where the list of participants included the Stead family along with British politician Lloyd George, the Countess of Warwick and a representative sent by British Prime Minister Herbert Asquith, while Mrs Stead received a message of condolence from Queen Alexandra, the Danish wife of King Edward VII.

When news of *Titanic*'s sinking sped across the world, Mr Stead's son, who was in Johannesburg, could only hope that his father had survived, but one thing he knew for sure was that his father would have been one of the last to leave the ship. Fireman George Kemish reported seeing him reading in the first-class smoking room, looking as if he had no intention of doing anything else. Steward Andrew Cunningham helped him into a life jacket, ignoring his grumbling that it was all nonsense. Others spoke of how he helped women and children into the lifeboats and gave his life jacket away before jumping into the ocean.

He was a journalist and much more than that. In fact, he was expected to receive the 1912 Nobel Peace Prize, an honour that plenty felt he had long deserved for his courageous journalism and the boundless energy he poured into making the world a better place. He had his enemies too, as was inevitable, but would not be silenced or cowed into submission. In 1876, he was instrumental in the renewed popularity of William Gladstone after attacking Benjamin Disraeli's government for doing nothing when Britain's ally Turkey massacred 12,000 Bulgarian Christians. Prime Minister Disraeli declared that the number of civilian deaths had been greatly exaggerated but Stead and Gladstone refused to let the matter drop and wrote extensively about the massacre, with Stead publicising his belief that Gladstone should be in charge again. Four year later, the 1880 elections saw Gladstone returned to power in his second term as prime minister.

Stead endured six months in prison thanks to a misguided effort to reveal the murky trade of child prostitution by arranging to purchase Eliza Armstrong, the thirteen-year-old daughter of a chimney sweep. He had allegedly discovered that the British government knew about the sale of young girls to brothels but the authorities feigned ignorance to protect wealthy clients. Part of his crusade involved four articles in the *Pall Mall Gazette*, the paper he edited, which proved so popular that the newspaper ran out of paper and had to borrow from a rival. His exploits may have inspired George Bernard Shaw, who also wrote for the *Gazette*, to write his play *Pygmalion* and name the female lead Eliza, although Shaw also referred to Stead as 'an utter philistine' and they were never friends. Stead wanted to force the Criminal Law Amendment Bill through Parliament and, thus, raise the age of consent from thirteen to sixteen years, which duly happened.

Stead is credited with modernising the Victorian newspaper by using interviews, photographs, eye-catching headlines and embarking on various campaigns. His was a 'new journalism' that wielded its truth through the mighty pen and, furthermore, he was the first editor to employ female journalists. Yet, he was not a saint; for instance, he wasn't above printing alternative facts for a greater good. Plus, there was the sticky matter of his spiritual beliefs. At his last dinner on *Titanic* it was said that he talked a lot about spiritualism and the occult. He was all for psychic research and believed he was in contact with the spirit of a woman he had met just before she died in 1890. But did he foresee the *Titanic* disaster?

He wrote two stories years earlier, the first in 1886, entitled, 'How the Mail-Steamer Went Down in the Mid-Atlantic, by a Survivor', was about a sinking ship with too few lifeboats to save its occupants. The second, 'From the Old World to the New', appeared in 1892, about a White Star Line ship, the *Majestic*, that avoids hitting an iceberg thanks to the warning of an Irish woman, a clairvoyant, who saw, in her mind's eye, a ship colliding with an iceberg.

After his death, his spiritual friends waited to hear from Mr Stead and were rewarded on 24 April 1912 when a Mrs Feldman informed the Convention of Spiritualists Association that he had been in touch to tell her he was happy. In fact, he made several appearances, including his announcement through medium Mrs Coates of Rothesay, on 3 May 1912, that he was glad to have helped, and prayed with, so many on *Titanic*. Ten years after he died, Estelle, his daughter published the immensely readable *The Blue Island: Experiences of a New Arrival Beyond the Veil*, which she said had been dictated by her father to a medium and covered his death and the afterlife.

7

ICONIC MUSIC AND ICONIC ORCHESTRAS

O n being asked to pick a song that they associate with the *Titanic*, many people would name the Christian hymn 'Nearer My God to Thee'. It was written by Sarah Flower Adams in 1841, in her Sunnybank home, in Essex, England, and is loosely based on Genesis 28:11-12 when Jacob falls asleep and dreams of a ladder that stretches all the way from earth to Heaven. God descends this ladder to speak to Jacob who, on waking, proclaims, 'Surely God was in this place but I did not know it'.

It is widely believed that the hymn was the last piece of music played by the first-class *Titanic* orchestra, led by violinist Wallace Hartley.

There are alternative musical versions of the hymn which may explain why telegrapher Harold Bride told a reporter from *The New York Times* that the last music he remembered hearing was the hymn 'Autumn'. After the sinking, a former colleague of Wallace Hartley, from the *Mauretania*, related a conversation that he'd had with the violinist when he asked him what he would do

A rarely seen photograph of Wallace
Hartley with the Bridlington Municipal
Orchestra, seated to the left of the
bandmaster, his precious violin in his hand.

if he found himself trapped on a sinking ship. Wallace, a Methodist, replied that he would gather the orchestra together and play his favourite hymn, 'Nearer My God to Thee'.

Before he boarded *Titanic*, Wallace had played on the Cunard Line ships *Mauretania* and *Lusitania* and was headhunted by White Star Line. What an opportunity it must have seemed, to be able to play on the biggest ship ever built, in front of some of the world's wealthiest and most distinguished passengers. Pianist Theodore Brailey and cellist Roger Bricoux left *Carpathia* to join Wallace's band on *Titanic*, boasting to a friend, 'We will soon be on a decent ship with decent grub.' One can only imagine the excitement as the eight musicians unpacked their belongings in their second-class cabins and put on their uniform, which was green, including their socks. Unlike most of the crew, they were not paid by White Star Line. Instead, they were contracted by Liverpool musical agents Messrs C.W. and F.N. Black, and it was the agency that was paid by the shipping company. For a monthly wage of six pounds and ten shillings they were expected to know every one of the 352 tunes in their songbook to satisfy any passenger requests.

When the ship hit the iceberg, the captain asked that Wallace and his orchestra continue to play music, to retain some normality. They played ragtime tunes and waltzes which must have initially helped to keep the atmosphere cheerful. Wallace had a great belief in the power of music. After the sinking, a friend of his, John Carr, who played on the *Celtic*, was quoted as saying:

I know he [Wallace] often said that music was a bigger weapon for
stopping disorder than anything on earth. He knew the value of the
weapon he had, and I think he proved his point.

So, they decided to keep playing even after moving outside where they could see lifeboats being released into the ocean, one after the other. Still, they played on. Many people would argue that it doesn't matter which piece of music they played last, the important thing was that they kept playing.

Only three of their eight bodies were ever recovered: thirty-year-old bassist John Frederick Preston Clarke, twenty-year-old violinist John Law Hume and thirty-year-old bandleader Wallace Hartley. Both Hume and Clarke were buried in Halifax, Canada, on 8 May. Wallace's body, recovered on 4 May, was brought back to Liverpool on SS *Arabic*, a smaller and older White Star Line ship. His father was there to take him home and the coffin was placed onto a horse-drawn hearse for the sixty-five-mile journey to Colne in Lancashire.

On the day of his funeral, over 30,000 strangers turned up to walk behind his coffin. In other words, the story of the brave orchestra spread fast. Wallace was buried in a small cemetery on the edge of Colne, to the sound of 'Nearer My God to Thee'. His headstone shows a violin and the opening notes of his favourite hymn.

Then, on 24 May, 473 musicians from seven different orchestras played a concert at the Royal Albert Hall, in London, in memory of Wallace and his friends. Six days later, on 30 May, Mr Hume,

John's father, received a letter from Black's agency, looking to be reimbursed for the loss of John's uniform. Apparently, this was standard practice at the time.

When Wallace Hartley's body was found by the crew of the *Mackay-Bennet* there was no mention of his violin but this may just have been an oversight. Therefore, when the violin went on sale in 2013, it naturally caused a tremendous stir amongst the *Titanic* world with plenty doubting its authenticity. Could this really be the instrument that played 'Nearer My God to Thee' as the ship was sinking? It required a thorough investigation which turned up the fact that the violin had been mentioned in four contemporary newspapers on two continents.

Furthermore, Wallace had been engaged to Maria Robinson who had given him the violin to celebrate their engagement and fortunately she kept a diary. The entry for 16 July 1912 is a draft of a letter for the secretary at Halifax in which she sends her thanks for the return of her late fiancé's violin.

Before it was sold, the instrument went on exhibition in America where it attracted over 300,000 people in just three months.

On 19 October 1913, Mr Alan Aldridge, the auctioneer at Henry Aldright & Sons, Devizes, Wiltshire, England, opened the bidding for the violin at £50. In a matter of minutes, that sum had jumped to £100,000. A fierce battle ensued between two phone bidders, but there could only be one winner, whichever of them that finally bought it for £900,000 ($1.7million). Mr Aldridge believed the buyer was British and that was all he would say on the matter.

Some people were surprised that it did not sell for more. What was on sale that day was more than an old violin; the instrument represented the most wonderful, inspiring story about eight ordinary men who decided to just keep playing music as the Atlantic Ocean lapped around their ankles and death was approaching. As Father Browne wrote about his short stay on *Titanic*:

> *After dinner we listened to that orchestra which, in a few days' time, was to win a place in history more tragically glorious than that held by many others of the tragedy of April 15.*

If pressed for a second song about the *Titanic*, Celine Dion's, 'My Heart Will Go On' might spring to mind. It is the theme song from James Cameron's 1997 *Titanic* film, with lyrics by Will Jennings and music by James Horner. Maybe the best thing about a hugely bestselling, international and iconic song is the fact that a lot of people can still dislike it. Celine Dion didn't think much of the song when it was first played to her. James Cameron didn't even want a theme song for his film and took an awful lot of persuading, in fact almost two months of persuading, including watching a preview audience, in New York, succumb to tears as the song played out the end of the film.

Meanwhile, Kate Winslet told an interviewer that she feels ill whenever she hears it. In any case, it made Celine Dion extremely rich, enabling her to turn down work and concentrate on motherhood. The song also won a pile of awards in 1998, including an

Oscar for 'Best Song from a Film' and four Grammys: 'Record of the Year'; 'Best Female Pop Vocal Performance'; 'Song of the Year'; 'Best Song from a Motion Picture.' With over 15 million singles sold, this song is the tenth bestselling record of all time.

WHAT WAS ON SALE THAT DAY WAS MORE THAN AN OLD VIOLIN ...

BRIDES, WIDOWS AND FAMOUS COUPLES

Lifeboat 7 was one of the first to be released. It was 12.40am and Officer Murdoch was supervising the loading. Few passengers realised the seriousness of the situation, at this early stage, and some struggled to believe that their salvation lay in disembarking *Titanic*, in the middle of the night, in a small, wooden lifeboat. Gesturing to the boat, Officer Murdock called out to the group in front of him, 'Ladies, this way!' No one moved and then, noticing that the crowd was mostly composed of young couples, someone shouted out, 'Put in the brides and grooms first!'

Of the twenty-one newly married couples on board, twenty brides found themselves widowed on the morning of 15 April 1912. Three of those couples are selected here.

MR AND MRS NICHOLAS NASSER

Only a few weeks married, *Titanic*'s youngest bride, fourteen-year-old Mrs Adele Nasser (1898–1970), of Syrian descent, was travelling in second class with her husband Nicholas (1884–1912). They were not the only newly married Syrian couple on board, but they were the only newly married Syrian couple not travelling in steerage thanks to Nicholas's confectionary business in Cleveland. He had worked hard for ten long years until he felt he had acquired enough to return to his homeland in search of a wife. Mrs Nasser was a few weeks into her first pregnancy and, later that year, gave birth to a son on 9 December, but the child died a few hours later. Nicholas's body was found by the *Mackay-Bennett* and was described in the report as being of 'Italian type', which was a typical description for anyone that looked foreign. His personal effects were listed as a watch and chain, a purse with £7 and a belt around his waist that held £160 in gold. On his right forearm was a tattoo of a lion with a sword. Why did he not press any money into his wife's hand before he said goodbye to her? Perhaps he believed that he would also be rescued, although the lifeboat carrying his wife was one of the last lifeboats to be released, at about 1.50am. After his wife left, he kept busy helping children into the other lifeboats.

Mrs Nasser (sometimes Nasrallah) had been forcibly taken from her husband's arms and placed into Lifeboat 4 whose occupants included Mrs John Jacob Astor, who tried to comfort the frightened girl but found it difficult to make herself understood due to the language barrier. Still, they must have got on at some level and unfortunately, they had plenty in common in that they were both in their teens and recently married, both pregnant and both had been reluctant to leave their much older husbands behind.

It is some coincidence that, afterwards, she and Mrs Astor's fortunes would collide once more when the body of Nicholas Nasser was briefly mistaken for that of Colonel John Jacob Astor.

Months later, Mrs Nasser wrote to Mrs Astor. The letter is remarkable for the fact that in it, Mrs Nasser claims to be twenty-one-years of age and that she had been married to Nicholas for three years. Perhaps she felt that fourteen-year-old brides were not the norm in America or maybe, for legal reasons, she was advised to add a few years onto her age. Had her husband made out a will before his marriage? Were there papers to be signed regarding his business? On arriving in New York, she was friendless, penniless and obliged to rely on a cousin of her husband's whose family took her in. She had to wait several months before the money found on her husband's body was released to her, while her pregnancy prevented her from getting a job. When she did give birth, Madeline Astor sent a telegram of congratulations. We don't know if Lady Astor was informed when the infant died a few hours later. There is no evidence to suggest that the two widows stayed in contact after that. Within a couple of years, both women had married again and went on to have seven children between them.

MR AND MRS LUCIEN SMITH

Another honeymoon to end in disaster was that of West Virginian couple twenty-four-year-old Lucien and eighteen-year-old

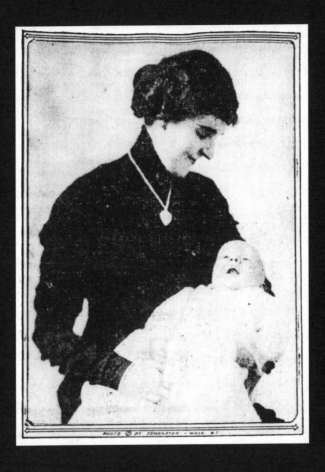

Eloise Smith with her son, Lucien, who was born
30 November 1912.

Mary Eloise Smith although there would be a happy ending, that is, a *temporary* happy ending involving fellow first-class passenger, Philadelphia banker Robert Daniel. The Smiths had married that February, in 1912, with a wedding that the local newspaper described as being 'most brilliant'. They then left for a honeymoon, travelling to Egypt, the Middle East and Europe. On discovering that Eloise was two months pregnant, they decided it was time to go home.

On *Titanic*, Eloise was woken up by her husband who casually informed her that the ship had struck an iceberg, and following protocol, the captain had requested all women up on deck. Because of Lucien's relaxed manner, his wife took her time dressing and was possibly one of the few women who dressed for the freezing temperatures, putting on a heavy dress, two coats, knitted hood and boots. On hearing that women and children were to be loaded into lifeboats, Eloise refused to leave and looked around for assistance. She spotted Captain Smith with a megaphone and was desperate enough to ask him if her husband could accompany her into the lifeboat, but the captain ignored her.

Lucien moved her away, begging her to go, but she steadfastly refused to be separated from him. Realising that he needed to lie, he told her that it was a precautionary requirement to have the women and children removed first. *Titanic* was thoroughly equipped, he assured her, and, therefore, nobody was going to die. Obviously, she wanted – and needed – so very much to believe him and asked if he was telling her the truth, to which he replied yes. He kissed her and led her to Lifeboat 6, suggesting she kept her hands in her pockets as it was such a chilly night. His body was never found. Afterwards, Eloise said that had she known there were not enough lifeboats, she would never have left him, and he must have known this which was why he lied to her. Eloise gave birth, on 30 November, to a son that she named after his father.

Virginian-born Robert Daniel had already tangled with disaster before he boarded *Titanic*, when he was obliged to save a friend's life after a fire broke out in their London hotel. He survived the sinking, though exactly how he did so remains a bit of a mystery. There is one account that has him swimming nude in the Atlantic for a couple of hours before he is rescued by a lifeboat, while Walter Lord writes that he was wearing woollen pyjamas. If he did end up in the water, a lifeboat stopped to rescue him. Meanwhile, *The New York Times* reported him taking over *Carpathia*'s wireless room for the journey back to New York. His day clothes were not the only items he left on *Titanic*. He had just bought himself a French bulldog but didn't try to save it, along with nearly $5,000 in cash. At some point, he met Eloise. Again, there are differing versions as to how, some have him jumping into her lifeboat, but she was in Lifeboat 6, while he managed, at the last moment, to end up in Lifeboat 4, Mrs Astor's boat. One story has him presenting himself to Eloise on *Carpathia* with the excuse that she is the only southern woman on board. Maybe he had already acquainted himself with the Smiths before *Titanic* hit the iceberg. In any case, upon reaching New York, it is he who carries the distraught widow off *Carpathia* and hands her over to her father, Congressman James Anthony Hughes. Presumably father and daughter leave immediately, but Robert was briefly interviewed by a reporter from the *Worcester Evening Gazette* who described him as being in good shape, wearing a raincoat but no tie. Robert said he was partially undressed at the time of the collision and ran up on deck to see what had happened. He also said that plenty of others just went back to bed.

Eloise's son was the second *Titanic* baby born after the sinking, and she received a telegram of congratulations from Mrs John Jacob Astor. Then she had an unpleasant situation with Lucien's family and brought them to court to recover part of his estate for their son. His relatives tried convincing her that there was no estate and that Lucien had been living on a monthly allowance of $500. They were not lying; Lucien came from a considerably wealthy family, but none of the money was his and he was, therefore, dependent on their generous allowance.

Robert Daniel obviously kept in touch because he and Eloise quietly married on 18 August 1914, in a private ceremony in New York, in complete contrast to the magnificent spectacle that was her first wedding. They wanted to avoid the journalists as best they could which proved easy enough when Robert had to leave the very next day for a three-week business trip to London. Unfortunately, however, he wound up stuck in London for the next two months due to the outbreak of war. How crucial were those first two months of marriage spent separated by the Atlantic

Ocean? He made it back to America a few weeks shy of Lucien Smith II's second birthday on 30 October. The toddler was a constant reminder of his wife's first love. One can only guess when the cracks began to show and why. The couple separated in 1918 and, in 1923, Eloise filed for divorce, citing an unknown blonde-haired woman who may have been Margery Pitt Durant, the woman Robert married that same year. His second marriage lasted five years before Margery filed for divorce. Robert married his third, and final, wife a year later in 1929. He died on 20 December 1940 from cirrhosis of the liver, seven months after the death of his first wife.

Eloise had also remarried in 1923, to a thirty-six-year-old wounded First World War veteran, Captain Lewis H Cort. The marriage lasted six years until the captain's premature death on 29 November 1929. Perhaps she felt that her second marriage was the best solution to help her get over the loss of her first husband and, if that is the case, Eloise repeats this method on the death of her third husband. However, this time, instead of the two-year gap between her first and second marriages, a mere twenty-one days passes before she weds Charles Wright on 20 December 1929. Her final marriage lasted four months with no public explanation for their divorce. She was thirty-seven years old and single for the first time in eighteen years, and it is now that she comes full circle, reverting to the name of her first husband, and finding a new occupation in touring the church halls of West Virginia to talk about the *Titanic* tragedy. Supposedly, she was planning to write her own book about the sinking before her heart attack, at forty-six years of age, on the morning 3 May 1940.

MR AND MRS JOHN JACOB ASTOR

When divorced forty-seven-year-old Colonel John Jacob Astor IV fell in love with and then married eighteen-year-old socialite Madeline Force, in September 1911, it caused a sensation. The terms of his divorce prevented him marrying in New York, where he lived, and it had been necessary to offer a reward of $1,000 to embolden a minister to officiate at the wedding. The upcoming

John Jacob Astor and his second wife, Madeline.

nuptials were frowned upon due to the age gap and their different circumstances. Her father was an industrialist and, therefore, his money was 'new', while John Jacob came from old money; his family were one of New York's finest and wealthiest, and had been for many years. The lengthy honeymoon to Egypt and Europe was an effort to escape the gossip and the journalists, and only came to an end when Madeline became pregnant. They boarded *Titanic* in Cherbourg to return to New York. John Jacob was the richest man on the ship and he undoubtedly made two women happy when *Titanic* docked beyond Queenstown. The ship was boarded by local vendors and the Colonel spent a small fortune on a lace shawl for Madeline.

Many remark on his calmness after *Titanic* hit the iceberg, and Madeline was not alarmed thanks to his composure. She was asleep when it happened, he woke her up, bid her get dressed and he had them both put on their life jackets. After that, they were seen in the gym, sitting on the mechanical horses, he had an extra life jacket in his lap that he had slit open to show how it was made. This may sound like a criminal waste, but there were 3,560 life jackets on board so the colonel's extra one would not have been needed. When they were faced with the prospect of the lifeboats, Colonel Astor demurred, believing that they'd be safer staying on *Titanic*. Finally, he accepted the situation and saw Lifeboat 4 through a window, pausing on its way down to the ocean, to take on more passengers. Colonel Astor helped Madeline to climb through the window and into the boat, asking the officer in charge – Officer Lightoller – if he could accompany his wife because of her 'delicate condition'. He was refused as the second officer was focused on saving the women and children only. The colonel checked the number of Madeline's boat – four – to be able to find her easily afterwards. Some have criticised him for trying to escape, but his wife was young and pregnant with her first child and was undoubtedly begging him to come with her. She hadn't mixed much with the other passengers, preferring to stay inside their suites, while he had been seen walking his dog Betty. One imagines that they caused a bit of excitement amongst their fellow passengers who would have known their back story.

Walter Lord credits Madeline with helping to save Daniel Buckley, a young Cork man and steerage passenger, who flung himself, along with a few other men into a lifeboat. Buckley says he curled up and wept as crew dragged the other men out, but they missed him thanks to a woman who hid him with her shawl. Buckley had always believed that it was Lady Astor who rescued him, but he was in Lifeboat 13.

There is a second story about Madeline and her shawl. On the boat deck, she found herself standing next to a Polish woman, Leah Aks, who was cradling her baby boy from the cold. Madeline gave or lent the child her shawl and we can only wonder if it was the lace shawl from Queenstown. In any case, she ends up in a different lifeboat from both mother and child, who are mistakenly separated when the baby is thrown into Lifeboat 11, and Leah is prevented from following him and is placed into Lifeboat 13. She was reunited with her son after seeing him in another woman's arms on *Carpathia* but needed Captain Rostron's help when the stranger refused to hand him over. The captain came up trumps and, out of gratitude, she decided to name her second baby, born in 1913, Sarah Carpathia Aks, but the nuns in the hospital made a mistake and filled out the forms with Sarah Titanic Aks.

His wife safe, Colonel Astor helped officers to fill the rest of the boats. A newspaper article on 20 April 1912 describes his last act, which was to place a baby in the last lifeboat. He stood watching the boat being lowered into the water and made a final gesture, saluting in farewell. Another story names him as the culprit behind releasing the dogs from their kennels. Eleven-year-old William Carter wanted to bring his dog with him into Lifeboat 4 and cried when he was prevented from doing so. Colonel Astor promised to take care of his pet and took the dog's leash.

In New York, Madeline was met by two cars carrying two doctors, a nurse, a secretary and Vincent, her husband's son from his first marriage. John Jacob Astor's body was found by the *Mackay-Bennett*. He had $2,500 in his pocket and was wearing a wire belt with a gold buckle, a family heirloom. It is Vincent who accepted his father's body, while Madeline held a solitary vigil beside the coffin. Colonel Astor was buried in Trinity Cemetery in New York on 5 May, and flowers were sent from England by King George.

Perhaps it is only natural that the papers dwelt on the colonel's wealth. There are many articles in 1912 about the net worth of *Titanic*'s lost millionaires and, on 8 May, the colonel's newest will was made public. Previously there was no mention of Madeline in the will made before their marriage but, of course, that had been amended. He left her an outright $100,000 along with their big house on Fifth Avenue and a trust fund worth $5 million. However, she would lose the latter two if she ever remarried. Madeline gave birth to their son in August and named him John Jacob. Six years later she gave up her claim to the Astor fortune by marrying William Dick, a wealthy childhood friend. They had two children, a boy and a girl. Years later, Madeline hired a young Italian boxer to train her teenage son and ended up leaving William for him, thereby giving up a second fortune. Unfortunately, this third marriage was a disaster, and possibly violent, and they divorced in 1938. Two years later Madeline was dead, at the age of forty-six, from a heart condition. She was buried with her mother in Trinity Church Cemetery, the final resting place of her first husband.

This cemetery would find itself at the heart of another disaster, albeit a very different kind, on 11 September 2001. St Paul's Chapel, part of Trinity Church, stood across the street from the Twin Towers and, therefore, should not have survived that day. Many of its neighbouring buildings sustained awful damage as the towers burned and collapsed. However, wreckage from the towers knocked over an almost century-old sycamore tree in the churchyard, causing it to fall across the church and shield it from the devastating debris. Instead of being destroyed, the church remained intact and provided shelter from the terror outside.

Isidor (seated front in white suit) and Ida (also seated front in dark dress) Straus, in 1905, with their children and grandchildren. This photograph was kindly supplied by the Straus Historical Society

THE COUPLE WHO DIED TOGETHER

There were many long-term married couples on board the ship, too many to mention here, some who refused to be parted one way or another. In hindsight, the husbands had two choices, to die or to be branded a coward.

The most famous *Titanic* love story is not James Cameron's fictional Rose and Jack, full of youth and vigour, but that of a wealthy middle-aged couple, travelling in first class, who refused to be parted or saved. German Jewish American Isidor Straus married German-born Rosalie Ida Blun in 1871 and by all accounts the match was an idyllic one. They had seven children and rarely spent a night apart.

In the mid-1890s, Isidor took over New York's Macy's Department Store and also served as a congressman thanks to his friendship with President Grover Cleveland.

In 1912, Mr and Mrs Straus travelled to Europe with Isidor's manservant, forty-nine-year-old John Farthing, from Suffolk, England. They first went to Cap Martin in France, where Mr Straus was recovering from an illness. After that, they visited family in Germany and went on to England, where Mr Straus tried to help resolve the coal strike. Mrs Straus had hoped to hire a French maid, but it was not to be and, just before the couple boarded *Titanic* in Southampton, she hired thirty-one-year-old English woman Ellen Bird.

We know what happened next thanks to several witnesses including Ellen, who survived the tragedy. She says that Mrs Straus was unsure about whether to get into a lifeboat or not, first handing Ellen some jewellery and then, her mind made up, taking it back again. She made the girl take her fur coat, saying that she wouldn't need it anymore, and then point-blank refused to go anywhere, telling her husband of forty-one years, 'Where you go, I go'. Consequently, Ellen was the lucky recipient of the seat in Lifeboat 8, while John Farthing would suffer the same fate as his employers. If Mrs Straus had made a different decision, one can only assume that she would have regretted it forevermore. Fellow passengers Colonel Gracie and Hugh Woolner suggested that the couple could both find space in a lifeboat owing to Mr Straus's age, but he refused to leave *Titanic* before any other man. They walked off together, side by side, content and at peace. Afterwards, Ellen tried to return her mistress's coat to Sarah, the eldest of the Straus children, but she was told to keep it because their mother obviously wanted her to have it. Ida's body was never recovered, while Isidor's was found by the *Mackay-Bennett*, brought to Nova Scotia where it was identified, and then shipped back to New York, where he was buried in Woodlawn Cemetery in the Bronx.

On 27 April 1912, the *Gettysburg Times* wrote an article declaring that 60,000 people in Jerusalem were fasting and mourning the Straus couple who had funded a soup kitchen that fed 500 daily, which was incorrect as it was Isidor's brother, Nathan, and his wife Lina, who opened the kitchen in 1912. Nathan and Lina visited Palestine in February 1912 and, then, on 12 April, they were in Rome, where Nathan was attending the International Tuberculosis Congress as an American delegate. Some sources wrongly claimed that the two brothers and their wives were travelling together which is a frustration for the Straus Historical Society.

An unusual footnote to their story was reported in *The New York Times* on Friday, 26 April. Six-year-old Bess was Mr Straus's favourite horse and, before the couple embarked on their trip, he had her sent to a farm in New York for a rest. On the morning of 15 April 1912, the healthy horse was found dead in her stable, the vet unable to give an explanation. However, the Straus Historical Society reminds us that both Straus brothers kept horses so this may or may not be true.

Today, in New York, you can visit Straus Memorial Park, not far from their home, to see the 1913 bronze sculpture of a reclining woman gazing at the water below and engraved with the words:

> In memory of Isidor and Ida Straus, lost at sea in the Titanic disaster … Lovely and pleasant were they in their lives, and in their death, they were not parted.

Mrs Straus was one of only four first-class women lost in the sinking.

THE COUPLE WHO SURVIVED TOGETHER

Sir Cosmo and his wife Lady Lucy Duff-Gordon are the most controversial *Titanic* couple and were the only passengers questioned at both the American and British hearings. He was her second husband as she had divorced her alcoholic first one. Thanks to the breakdown of that marriage, Lucy established herself as a career woman, creating a business out of her girlhood love for fashion. Initially setting up shop in her house, she then acquired proper premises, Maison Lucille, in West London, and soon after that an even bigger shop, gradually spawning a small chain across Europe and America. She was famous for her lingerie, tea gowns and evening wear and looked after royalty, actresses and ballet dancers. Lady Hazel Lavery, the American wife of Belfast painter John Lavery, who was described by the *New York Tribune*, as being the most beautiful American woman living in England, modelled

Right: Lady Lucy-Duff Gordon, proprietor of successful fashion house Maison Lucille.

Sir Cosmo Duff-Gordon who underwent a grilling at the British investigation into the sinking.

Lucile gowns for magazines such as *Tatler's*. However, even her business would provide its own brand of controversy when she admitted that she did not design most of the dresses she sold from 1911 onwards. Aside from that, she is supposedly the first person to train professional models and the catwalk show was her invention. In 1900, she married Eton-educated Cosmo Duff-Gordon, a baron, who became a director of her company Lucile Ltd. Six years later, he fenced for Britain at the Intercalated Games (a sort of intermediary Olympic games), taking the silver in a team event.

In 1912, they boarded *Titanic* to visit the New York branch of Lucille, travelling under the aliases Mr and Mrs Morgan, possibly to escape the magazine diarists. With them was Miss Francatelli, Lady Duff-Gordon's secretary. Ironically, the Duff-Gordon name would be dragged every which way through the press for months after the sinking. Sir Cosmo is one of the few men from first class to survive the tragedy. According to him, both his wife and her secretary refused to leave him, allowing two lifeboats to take off without them. Finally, they found themselves in front of Lifeboat 1, one of the smaller boats with a capacity for forty passengers, and, after standing there for a while, waiting for orders, Sir Cosmo asked the officer in charge if he could accompany the two women. First Officer William Murdoch allegedly replied, 'Oh, certainly do, I will be very pleased.' This seems like an overly solicitous response on Murdoch's part when you consider that the richest man on board, Colonel Astor, was prevented from accompanying his pregnant wife and, of course, the first officer did not live to corroborate the story. It highlights the confusion amongst the crew and officers regarding whether Captain Smith meant women and children were to be dealt with first or they were the only ones to be saved. In that case, Officers Lightoller and Murdoch could have been following their personal interpretation of the order to fill the lifeboats.

The Duff-Gordons and Miss Francatelli got into the boat along with leading Fireman Charles Hendrickson, who later explained his own presence and that of several other firemen, by saying that no one answered the officer when he had called out, looking for seamen to take the oars. A call had also been made for women and children but there were none about. At the British inquiry into the tragedy, Lord Mersey, the leading investigator, was much caught by the fact that this lifeboat was sent into the ocean with just twelve people on board, five passengers – two women and three men – and seven crew. He was told repeatedly that, at the time of its release, there was no one else around which is remarkable considering that Lifeboat 1 was only launched at 1.05am. Lifeboat 7, the first one, was launched at 12.40am, from starboard, and just two boats separated it from Lifeboat 1, and, in Boat 7 a mere twenty-eight passengers left in a boat that should have contained sixty-five. At 12.40am, the sailors were mostly dealing with people reluctant to exchange the biggest ship in the world for a lifeboat. This is probably one of the boats that Lady Duff-Gordon and her secretary refused to enter. Still, can we believe that thirty minutes later there is nobody around Lifeboat 1? By this stage, Lord Astor has pointed out *Titanic*'s listing to one side which convinces Sir Cosmo that it might be sensible to go. Yet, the claim of absent passengers is first aired at the American investigation by first-class passenger Henry Stengel, who was also in Lifeboat 1. This investigation preceded the British one by a few weeks, starting the day after the survivors arrived in New York, and was led by the Republican lawyer Senator William Alden Smith. Stengel described how he got his wife into Lifeboat 5, and on spotting Lifeboat 1, approached and asked if he could get in. He remembered it being too dark to see much, and the only people around were the sailors working the boats. Is this further confirmation of the mistakes made by the crew that night that passengers were not being properly directed towards all the lifeboats?

Meanwhile, matters regarding the Duff-Gordons took a murky turn. Back in London, Fireman Robert William Pusey testified that on *Titanic*'s disappearing into the ocean, he heard Lady Duff-Gordon

Sir Cosmo (centre, back row) and Lady Duff-Gordon (in furs), their secretary and the crew of Lifeboat 1 caused upset on *Carpathia* in posing for this photograph with so many still to be rescued'

say, 'There is my beautiful nightdress gone.' In *A Night to Remember*, Walter Lord has her direct the comment to her secretary, 'There is your beautiful nightdress gone.' Obviously, it doesn't matter whose nightdress is lost but, to the modern ear, it sounds callous and unfeeling. However, when one reads her replies to Lord Mersey, Lady Duff-Gordon did appear oblivious to over 1,500 people either dead or dying in the water or still on board the sunken ship. Unsurprisingly, the remark irritated her fellow passengers and the crew, and Fireman Pusey reminded her that she was lucky to be alive.

The hearings of the British Wreck Commissioner's Inquiry opened in Westminster, London, on 2 May 1912. Lord Mersey had been chosen to lead the investigation by the British Board of Trade, and the court room was packed for the Duff-Gordon episode with an excited audience that included Count Prince Leopold of Battenburg, Prince Albert of Schleswig-Holstein and Count Benckendorff, the Russian Ambassador. It was around this time that the press began to refer to Lifeboat 1 as the 'Money Boat' thanks to the conversation initiated by Lady Duff-Gordon's regret over a lost nightdress. Once the court had dealt with the boat being launched with just twelve passengers, there was the bewildering fact that this practically empty boat did not turn back to try to rescue anyone. This was a sticking point for Senator Smith, in the American investigation, and an even bigger one for Lord Mersey who positively grilled Fireman Hendrickson and Sir Cosmo in this respect and remained unsatisfied with their explanations. Hendrickson claimed that he proposed returning to save people to which the men said nothing while the two women – Lady Duff-Gordon and her secretary – objected, saying it was too dangerous because the boat would be swamped. Lord Mersey demanded that the fireman clarify his answer that no attempt was made to rescue anyone on account of the two women but not before checking whether Sir Cosmo had 'reproved' his wife for her attitude. The answer was negative, that her husband had agreed with her. Lord Mersey asked again what everyone else said about going back and this time Hendrickson replied that it was the two Duff-Gordons who said they should not return, while no one else ventured an opinion.

This problem about not turning back was compounded by that unfortunate conversation. In Lifeboat 1, about thirty minutes after Pursey snapped at Lady Duff-Gordon over her nightdress comment, he followed it up by asking Sir Cosmo if he had lost everything too and, when the baron said yes, Pursey was at pains to point out that whatever the Duff-Gordons had lost, they had the means of replacing it, while he and the rest of the crew had lost their kit and would not be given a new one, and, furthermore, their pay would have been stopped that very night. Perhaps it was an instinctive reflex on Sir Cosmo's part, but he immediately offered the men a cheque for £5 each towards the price of a new kit. In the aftermath of the sinking some then wondered if this kindly gesture had been a means of bribing the men to keep rowing away from those in peril. Both Pursey and Henrikson denied this, saying that the cheque was a pleasant surprise. Lord Mersey queried exactly when Sir Cosmo had promised them this gift, and they both answered that they had first heard mention of it on *Carpathia*.

On 24 April, the *Newark Star* published an interview with Mr Stengel in which he said that initially the men, including the firemen and seamen, did not work as they should, that they lay down in the boat, smoked cigarettes and made jokes, prompting Sir Cosmo to announce that he would make them all a gift if they took care of them – meaning the other occupants. His wife, who wasn't feeling well, added that she had some money on her, while Sir Cosmo handed out cigars. Mr Stengel alluded to a second round of gifts made on *Carpathia* but he didn't know the amount involved. The journalist told him that Sir Cosmo had been quoted as saying that they had sung hymns together to keep their spirits up and deafen themselves to the wails of the dying. This was rejected by Stengel who repeated that the men that should have been rowing were laughing and joking. Senator Smith does not mention the issue of bribery during the American investigation, probably because he knew nothing about it.

Sir Cosmo had a rough time in the dock with Lord Mersey who forced him to admit that he had heard the cries of people dying. When Sir Cosmo was asked if it had occurred to him that he could save somebody, he made a weak reply, that it was difficult for him to say because he was too busy caring for his wife and there was too much else to think about. Lady Duff-Gordon was suffering from a bad bout of seasickness yet there were no waves that night – the sea had been compared to a sheet of glass – or had conditions changed since *Titanic* hit the iceberg? Or maybe Lady Duff-Gordon wasn't sick at this point, maybe that happens later? Or is it the case that following an approximate seventy minutes of rowing, that any group of people who are relieved to have escaped death, might well silently agree to keep going because they feel overwhelmed by the devastating situation being signalled by over a 1000 desperate people screaming for help in the distance behind them? Hendrickson said he alone proposed turning back but no one else in the boat remembered him saying anything.

On Thursday, 31 July, *The Times* printed Lord Mersey's *Titanic* Report in which he wrote that the charges of bribery made against Sir Cosmo Duff-Gordon were unfounded. He judged that, had the crew made the effort, they probably would have been able to save lives but he did not believe that they had been prevented from doing so by Sir Cosmo. However, he did believe that the men would have tried had Sir Cosmo encouraged them to return and, if they had, they could have saved some lives.

Lady Duff-Gordon escaped another fatal sea journey when, in May 1915, she booked herself onto *Lusitania* but was too ill to board. This was the ship's final journey when it was torpedoed by the Germans a few miles off the Irish coast. She published her autobiography *Discretions and Indiscretions* in 1932, Sir Cosmo had died the year before on 20 April 1931, and she maintained that the negative press and the charge of cowardice – for surviving when so many women and children had not – broke his heart and he never recovered from it. She died on 20 April 1935, on the fourth anniversary of her husband's death, and twenty-three years and five days after they survived the sinking of *Titanic*.

In 2011, journalist and writer Senan Molony wrote about the behaviour of those manning the *Titanic* lifeboats. He makes the case that the sailors in the lifeboats kept their vessels shrouded in darkness so as not to attract the attention of those in the water, that is, they decided against using their lamps. He quotes Samuel Hemming, a lamp trimmer, who, as *Titanic* foundered, followed Captain Smith's orders by personally lighting all the lamps and placing one in every lifeboat. The article can be found on Encyclopedia-Titanica's website; it makes for interesting reading.

9

SPORTING HEROES

THE TENNIS PLAYERS

Two gifted tennis players were on board the ship, though they would not meet one another until after being rescued by *Carpathia*. Swiss-born, twenty-one-year-old Richard (Dick) Norris Williams II and his father, Charles Duane Williams, were on their way to New York, where Richard was playing in various tennis tournaments before taking his place at Harvard University. His *Titanic* experience was considerably more dramatic and harrowing than that of fellow tennis player Karl Behr. Travelling in first class, father and son left their stateroom on C deck after the crash. On their way, they saw a steward struggling to free a panicked passenger from the other side of a locked door. Richard slammed his shoulder to the door and broke it open, for which he found himself threatened with legal action by the steward for

Right top: Tennis player Karl Behr boarded *Titanic* in pursuit of the girl he would later marry.
Right bottom: Tennis player Richard Norris Williams saw his father die in front of him.

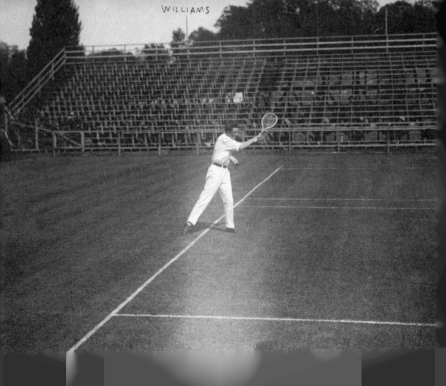

WILLIAMS

Above: Two years after surviving the sinking, Richard (Dick) Norris Williams II (second from left) and Karl Behr (second from right) played on the winning team in the 1914 Davis Cup.

damaging White Star Line property.

The two men went to the bar around midnight, to find it was closed. They asked another steward if he could open it for them but were told it was against regulations. So, they wandered about, watching some lifeboats being launched. Even with Richard in his fur cloak, they must have decided it was too cold to stay outside and headed to the gym, joining the group gathered there with instructor Thomas McCauley. One can't help wondering if the folk in the gymnasium truly appreciated that *Titanic* was sinking.

During *Titanic's* last moments, the fifty-one-year-old father and his son dived from the boat deck into the water, where Richard came face to face with Robert Daniel's prize bulldog. He shook off his shoes and fur coat. What happened next must have been devastating but it did save his own life. *Titanic's* forward funnel smashed down upon the people in the water. Richard narrowly avoided being crushed but saw his father disappear, along with many others, beneath the massive pipe. At the same time, the funnel, on impact with the water, created a wave that rushed Richard towards Collapsible A which he clung to for a while before being dragged into it. Unfortunately, the small, canvas boat had taken in water due to its faulty sides refusing to be raised, and Richard was forced to stand up to his waist in freezing water for the next nine hours or so. There were about thirty people in that boat but by the time Officer Lowe came to their rescue in his bigger Lifeboat 14, only eleven were still alive, the rest having succumbed to the cold and Richard's legs were purple in colour.

On *Carpathia*, the ship's doctor fretted about the tennis player's legs, wondering if he should amputate them. Richard vehemently disagreed, explaining that he needed them – and so he did. Six weeks later, he played and won a tennis tournament.

Twenty-six-year-old Karl Behr had represented the USA in the 1907 Davis Cup Final and, in the same year, lost the doubles final at Wimbledon. The reason he was on *Titanic* was that the love of his life, nineteen-year-old Helen Newsom, a friend of his sister, was on board. Her parents had attempted to break up their relationship by whisking Helen off on a tour of Europe, but Karl concocted a business trip to Europe and booked his return ticket for *Titanic* on hearing that his girlfriend and parents had booked theirs. One wonders at the reception he initially experienced when he presented himself to Helen on the ship. After the collision, Karl, who knew where the lifeboats were, led Helen's family to the deck with another couple, Mr and Mrs Edwin Kimball. After watching the first lifeboat make its descent to the water, they were directed towards the second one, Lifeboat No. 5. Mrs Kimball asked White Star Line director Bruce Ismay, who was helping to fill the boat, if their men could accompany them and Ismay quietly replied, 'Why certainly, Madam'. Nobody challenged this, and Behr ended up in the boat with Helen and her parents. Because there was still plenty of room, Third Officer Herbert Pitman and three other crew got in too, though Pitman stood and called in vain for more women to come forward. Not believing that the ship was going to sink, Pitman exited the boat but was ordered by First Officer Murdoch to take command of it.

On *Carpathia*, Behr did what he could to help the survivors and also joined a committee made up of grateful survivors who planned to honour *Carpathia*'s Captain Rostron and his crew for saving their lives. This they did later in New York, presenting the captain with a silver cup and his 320-strong crew with silver medals. Meanwhile, Richard Williams kept walking the deck to kick start the circulation in his legs and was grateful to Karl for keeping him company on those walks. The two men became firm friends and later, in 1912, they faced one another on court in a fierce fourth-round match for the Longwood Challenge Bowl. Behr won 0-6, 7-9, 6-2, 6-1, 6-4.

A year later, in March 1913, Karl and Helen got married and started a family.

Richard Williams went on to win the Davis Cup five times, the

US Nationals twice and the Wimbledon doubles. There is a wonderful photograph of them standing closely side by side after their American team won the Davis Cup in 1914.

Both men were inducted into the International Tennis Hall of Fame, Richard in 1957 and Karl, posthumously, in 1969.

THE SQUASH PLAYER

The game of squash was allegedly invented in 1830 by students at Harrow who discovered the skill required in using a racquet to hit – or squash – a punctured ball against a brick wall. The first courts were built at Harrow in 1864 thereby establishing squash as a proper sport. However, squash was not a popular spectator sport in 1912. Squash doubles did not come into its own until the 1930s which explains why most of *Titanic's* passengers would not have recognised second-class passenger Briton Charles Eugene Williams as the reigning world champion who was going to America to defend his title and win the $5,000 prize money.

On the night of the 14 April, Charles played squash until 10.30pm. *Titanic's* two deck high and 30-feet-long racquet squash court was in the lower deck. At approximately 10.30pm, Charles went to the smoking room where, just over an hour later, he heard a crash. He rushed out onto the deck and saw the iceberg, judging it to be 100 feet in height. There is no record of whether he knew anyone else on board. Afterwards, Charles told reporters that he made his way to the boat deck on the starboard side, from where he jumped off *Titanic*, striving to jump as far as he could from the sinking ship and then swim as fast as he could. He was picked up by Lifeboat 14, in which he spent nine hours standing up to his knees in freezing water. The sailors, he added, 'conducted themselves admirably'. It is interesting to note that his version of being rescued from the freezing water clashes with the officer in charge of the lifeboat, Fifth Officer Harold Godfrey Lowe, who said that he chose Charles back on deck to help him row the boat. Nobody could blame the sportsman if he preferred people to think he only survived because he was pulled out of the water as opposed to stepping into a lifeboat with ease.

Charles was to have played George E Standing in New York and it is thanks to George that we know the following story. He told a reporter from the *New York World* that Charles described how he threw himself overboard and spent two hours in the water before ending up in a lifeboat. Lowe's testimony contradicts this story and, really, to have spent that amount of time in the freezing water – and lived to tell the tale – sounds incredible unless Charles had been drinking lots of brandy or whiskey in the smoking room. According to George, Charles saw Captain Smith swimming around with a baby in his arms. When a lifeboat went to the captain's assistance, he handed over the infant but refused to get in himself. It is difficult to credit this story when we doubt Charles's claim to swimming in the Atlantic for a couple of hours.

THE BOXERS

There were two Welsh boxers on the ship. Twenty-one-year-old David 'Dai' Bowen, from Treherbert, Glamorgan was the Welsh Lightweight Champion. Married, he and his wife lived with his widowed mother. Before the tragedy, David wrote a letter to his mother from *Titanic* in which he described the ship as being bigger than Treherbert. He was travelling on the same third-class ticket with friend and boxing colleague Leslie Williams, a husband and father of one, who was from Tonypandy.

They were both responding to the chance of a lifetime when a Pennsylvanian promoter provided a twelve-month contract for two 'small' boxers to come and fight a series of contests in America. They had done well to be selected. When the offer first appeared in the 21 January 1911 edition of *Boxing*, sports journalist Charles Barnett, tasked with making the selection, wrote that he had two lightweights in mind and found himself inundated with applications from young boxers hoping to be selected. However, nothing happened because Barnett's favourites were too busy to make the journey and the 1911 boxing season ended. The following year, in February 1912, Barnett wrote that the promoter had added more money to the pot. Four weeks later, he confirmed that he had selected Bowen and Williams. The journalist had expected them to travel earlier than they did, possibly on *Lusitania*, but Williams needed more time to have new suits made, and Barnett did not want them travelling alone. In his column, he wrote about the great send-off that Treherbert Sports Club had given Bowen along with a fancy travelling bag that had been presented to him by the local Constitutional Club. The two boxers, he added, promised him that they would make plenty of use of *Titanic*'s gym to be fighting fit by the time they reached America.

Yet, however thrilled the two young men were, it must have been quite a wrench to leave their homes and families for an entire year. Williams wrote to his wife several times from *Titanic* and, in one letter, complained about the food, saying it was only good enough for ducks.

Both boxers died. Bowen's body was never found while Williams' was but it was not brought home. Instead, he was buried at sea a week after the sinking. It is not difficult to read the horror between the lines of Charles Barnett's response, printed in *Boxing* on April 27:

It seems but a moment ago since the two young boxers gripped my hand in farewell from the train which took them to Southampton. What a strange fate!

THE GYM MASTER

Titanic's gymnasium was on the boat deck, on the starboard side of the second funnel. With white panelled walls, this room had the best equipment available at the time: machines for weights, rowing and cycling, along with an electric camel and horse. The cycling

Thomas McCawley looking at home in his gym aboard *Titanic*.

machine sat in front of a huge wall clock that measured the distance and speed of the cyclist, while using the rowing apparatus allowed one to study the only pictures, either the map of the world crisscrossed with White Star routes or an illustrated guide to the ship's decks. This was physical educator's Thomas W McCauley's little kingdom. From Southampton, Thomas was reputed to have been quite strict with the adult passengers but kind and patient with the children who visited his gym. One shilling per visit was the entrance fee. Women could use the gym between 9.00am and 1.00pm; children's hours were between 1.00pm and 3.00pm, while the men took the last four hours of the day, 2.00pm to 6.00pm.

Thomas stayed in his gymnasium as the ship sank, where he explained his refusal to wear a life jacket. He had every confidence in being able to swim clear of the ship and believed that the jacket would only slow him down. His body was never found.

Father Browne, who had been ordered to leave the ship at Queenstown, must have treasured the business card that Thomas had given him. One can only guess what kind of conversation entailed between the priest and the gym instructor that prompted Thomas to give Father Browne his card. Possibly Thomas had more time on his hands, before the priest's final stop, in that it might take interested passengers a day or two to start availing of the gym. Therefore, Thomas may have taken the priest on a grand tour of the machines and, of course, he had his photograph taken too. After the sinking, Father Browne wrote about the fancily printed card of Mr T. W. McCawley. Printed in the bottom left-hand corner of the card is Thomas's 'address': The Gymnasium, R.M.S Titanic, White Star Line.

When one considers the photographs taken of *Titanic*'s crew, few show us the individual in their work place. Thanks to Father Browne, however, we can see Thomas sitting proudly on his rowing machine. He wasn't a tall man, but his shoulders, thick arms and chest suggest pure muscle and strength. Dressed head to toe in white, with neatly cropped hair and moustache; he is the perfect advertisement for any gym.

10

· · ·

HEROIC CLERGYMEN

Not counting Father Browne who disembarked at Queenstown, there were three Catholic priests and five Protestant reverends on board the ship. It is hardly surprising to learn that none survived, not one of them choosing to save themselves in place of others.

THE PRIESTS

The priests were Lithuanian Father Juozas Montvila (twenty-seven), who was fleeing Tsarist oppression of Catholics in the Ukraine, German Josef Benedikt Peruschitz (forty-one) and British Thomas Roussel Byles (forty-two). They were all involved in helping women and children into lifeboats and they did not take up the offer of a

Father Byles, a 'martyr for the church', according to Pope Pius X.

lifeboat seat for themselves. None of their bodies were ever found.

Yorkshire born, Father Byles was going to New York to offici-ate at his brother William's wedding. At the time, it was believed that to cancel a wedding brought bad luck so the ceremony went ahead, on a much smaller scale than originally planned, and after-wards the bride and groom visited *Titanic* survivors in St Vincent's hospital to find out about Father Byles's last hours. He had held mass on the morning of 14 April and preached a sermon about the new life that lay ahead for most of the passengers.

Following the collision, he was on deck helping people in what-ever way he could. Twice he was offered a lifeboat seat and twice he refused it. Possibly realising what lay ahead, he made his way down to the steerage passengers, offering his blessing and encour-aging them to be calm. Some say he led steerage passengers up to the boat deck, helping women and children into lifeboats, whisper-ing words of comfort to all who needed it. Survivor Bertha Moran, one of the third-class passengers that Father Byles put into a life-boat, heard the priest calmly reciting the rosary and the remaining passengers make their response even as her boat was rowed away from the sinking ship.

Near the end, as the stern began to stand up out of the water, Father Byles said the Act of Contrition before a crowd of a hun-dred or more – of all religions, who knelt in ocean water – and gave them absolution. Months later, William Byles and his wife travelled to Rome for a private audience with Pope Pius X who called Thomas 'a martyr for the church'.

Today, there is a campaign underway to have Father Byles canonized. A website has been set up in his name that provides a special prayer to be said for his beatification. However, any candidate for sainthood needs miracles in his name and, therefore, anyone who has prayed to Father Byles and feels that they have received an ample sign in reply are asked to email their testimony.

We can only assume that had Father Browne and his camera remained on the *Titanic*, both would have been lost. We should be grateful to his uncle Robert Browne, Bishop of Cloyne, because he was the one who surprised him with the gift of a two-day trip, in first class, on the newest and biggest ship in the world. His journey began with a train from Waterloo Station, London, to Southampton, from where he boarded *Titanic* for Cherbourg and, then, Queenstown where he disembarked. It was also this same uncle who presented the seventeen-year-old Francis with his first camera so that he could take photographs of his trip to Europe, after which he would enter the Jesuit order. Today, Father Browne is recognised as one of Ireland's most famous photographers. A collection of 42,000 negatives were found after his death in 1960 and several books of his work have been published as a result. His most celebrated photographs are probably those he took documenting his journey to, and on, *Titanic*. He allows us to imagine the chill in Waterloo Station on the morning of 10 April and then, the following day, see the telegraphist Jack Phillips on his twenty-fifth birthday. Phillips was to stay at his radio, until water swirled around his ankles, desperately searching for help. Father Browne took many photographs of *Titanic*, her decks, her cabins, her luxurious first-class facilities, but he was also interested in her crew and passengers. Not surprisingly, four days after he stepped off the ship, these pictures propelled his artistry onto the front pages of newspapers all over the world and they also literally sustained him as a photographer when Kodak supplied him with free camera film for the rest of his life.

THE REVERENDS

The five reverends were Robert James Bateman (fifty-two), Ernest Courtenay Carter (fifty-four), Scottish pastor John Harper (thirty-nine), Scottish Presbyterian Charles Leonard Kirkland (fifty-two) and Finnish William Lahtinen (thirty-five). Of the five of them, the only body recovered was that of Reverend Bateman. He is

Reverend William Lahtinen and his wife Anna.

buried in Evergreen Cemetery, Jacksonville, Florida.

On the evening of 14 April, Reverend Ernest Courtenay Carter conducted a hymn service in the second-class dining room. He was with his wife of twelve years, Lilian; they had no children. When the service finished at 10pm, the participants enjoyed the refreshments laid on by the staff, while Reverend Carter remarked that he hoped it was not the last time that hymns were sung on *Titanic*. After the collision, the reverend and Mrs Carter were offered a seat together in a lifeboat, but both refused, choosing to remain on the sinking ship.

Reverend William Lahtinen was travelling with his wife, Anna, and her sister, Lyyli Silvén, whom they were helping to emigrate to America, where they were already settled. Married in 1905, the childless couple adopted a baby, Martha Agnes, in 1907. Just four weeks before they boarded *Titanic*, five-year-old Martha took ill and died. It is, therefore, no surprise that her grieving parents would not be parted. After following her sister into a lifeboat, Anna changed her mind and returned to William. Lyyli Silvén remained in the boat and never forgot how nervous Anna looked, while William calmly smoked a cigar. Neither of the bodies were found.

What is commonly known as the '*Titanic* Bible' is the bible that belonged to second-class passenger Reverend Robert James Bateman. In the original Greek, the King James Version (KJV) edition survives thanks to the reverend handing it to his sister-in-law, Mrs Ada E Balls, just before she got into a lifeboat. Londoner Ada, a widow, was working as a parlour maid, and her brother-in-law convinced her to return to America with him, for a better life, with her two teenage sons to join her at a later date.

The bible is on display in the Upper Room Museum in Nashville, Tennessee. In the 9 April 1935 edition of the *Western Daily Press and Bristol Mirror*, there is an article about Reverend Bateman, in which family friend Arthur Pepler states that he believes that the reverend was the reason the orchestra played 'Nearer my God to Thee' in *Titanic*'s final moments. He explained that Reverend Bateman had recently returned on *Olympic* from Florida, where he conducted his missionary work, to put a headstone on his mother's grave. On *Titanic*, Captain Smith asked him to conduct the service that Sunday night that concluded with the reverend's favourite hymn, 'Nearer My God to Thee.' After he placed his sister-in-law in a lifeboat, he gave her his necktie to help keep her warm and told her, 'If I don't meet you again in this world, we will in the next!' On reading reports about a grey-haired man, standing with bowed head, beside the band, as they played 'Near my God to Thee', Arthur Pepler was convinced it was Reverend Bateman and that he had made a final request to hear his favourite hymn. An article in the *Baltimore Sun*, in 2012, described how the hymn was banned from the chapel in Maryland Masonic Grand Lodge, Hunt Valley, where Ada Balls lived from 1953 until her death in 1967. Noticing that she cried every time it was played, her chaplain asked her why and on hearing about her *Titanic* experience, the hymn was never played again.

Even in the Atlantic Ocean, Reverend Harper did his best to

convert his fellow passengers. He swam around asking people to open their hearts to Jesus. One young man was clinging on to a piece of debris, and when Reverend Harper asked him if he was saved, the man replied 'No!' whereupon the clergyman took off his life jacket and gave it to him saying, 'Here then, you need this more than I do'. The man was one of six lucky people to be rescued by a lifeboat. Another account has Reverend Harper running about the ship, shouting, 'Women, children and the unsaved in the lifeboats'; in other words, believers were already saved and, therefore, ready to die.

EVEN IN THE ATLANTIC OCEAN, REVEREND HARPER DID HIS BEST TO CONVERT HIS FELLOW PASSENGERS. HE SWAM AROUND ASKING PEOPLE TO OPEN THEIR HEARTS TO JESUS.

11

• • •

MORGAN ROBERTSON
- GENIUS OR PSYCHIC?

After *Titanic* sank, some people accused Morgan Robertson of being clairvoyant, while others wondered if he had conversed with God himself. Born in 1861, in Oswego, New York, to a sea captain father, the young Morgan developed an early passion for life at sea. However, after serving in the Merchant Marine between 1877 and 1886, he left it behind forevermore. From the vastness of the open water he turned his attention to minute objects, spending ten years as a diamond setter until his failing eyesight propelled him to find another way to make a living. A reporter gave him a book, a sea story written by Rudyard Kipling that, from an experienced seaman's point of view, was full of inaccuracies and this spurred Morgan to write his own. In 1898, he released his novella *Futility*, about the 'practically unsinkable' *Titan*, a massive new British liner that hits an iceberg at top speed and sinks in the North Atlantic on an April night with a huge loss of life because there were not enough lifeboats. You can imagine the curiosity roused when his novella was reissued in 1912

Morgan Robertson

and renamed, *The Wreck of the Titan*. One wonders if there was any criticism at the publisher's blatant attempt to cash in within months of the tragedy.

However, this wasn't the only time that Morgan inadvertently played prophet. His 1914 short story, 'Beyond the Spectrum', was about America and Japan going to war after Japan launched a surprise attack. In the story, Morgan describes a weapon of ultraviolet light that blinds and burns men, just like the atomic bomb that only made its first appearance in 1945.

Scroll back a few years to 1905, when he released his novel, *The Submarine Destroyer*, which contains what is supposedly the first mention of a periscope in fiction. In fact, Morgan claimed to have invented the periscope but was refused a patent for it. Simon Lake, a naval architect, had been using them in his submarines since 1902 which explained Morgan receiving no credit for the instrument.

He never made much money from his writing and was not afraid to show his frustration. In his four-page autobiography, for the *Saturday Evening Post*, which was reprinted in the monthly periodical *McClure's Magazine* in 1916, a year after he died, Morgan referred to himself as a rolling stone that gathered no moss. He spoke of writing over 200 short stories and appearing in every major publication in America and some English ones too. He had written fourteen novels, none of which had sold for more than a dollar. He would see them in his local library, his entire repertoire of books, explaining how he had to use the library because he could not afford to buy new books. He put it out there, 'I'm broke!' adding that he was not a spendthrift, owned one good suit and had never made more than $5,000 in any one year. Only God knows what he would make of the prices that are being charged today for first editions of *The Wreck of the Titian*. In 2011, an American bookseller claimed he would not be selling his copy for less than $10,000, while in 2014, an 1898 edition of *Futility* sold for £4,272.

Following his death, a group of his friends got together to write a book about 'Morg' as they called him. *Morgan Robertson, The Man* is a moving and affectionate tribute; he was much loved. One of them describes that after years of stressing over his financial woes his books began to sell. He was in good spirits, though his health was flagging, so his friends suggested that he take himself away to Atlantic City for a break. His body was discovered standing upright, his hand resting on an oak dresser and the open window allowing his face to be caressed by the sea breeze, which was apt as he had recently announced his plan to return to the sea once more.

One of his friends, J O'Neill, an artist, wrote a piece for the book in which he extolled Morgan's writing as being the happy result of mediumship. He described Morgan's writing process, his ideas only occurred while he was half-asleep and, therefore, he began his working day in a horizontal position to achieve this state. Ideas and words would slowly converge until a narrative was spawned, necessitating a rush to his typewriter to type what had been dictated to him. There was a snag in that the narrative usually fell short and he would break off from typing, not knowing what came next. He had no recourse but to wait for the rest of the story to befall him and that could take weeks or months. Meanwhile, Morgan fretted about money which hindered proceedings. He took to reading psychology books in search of a remedy and this, O'Neill explained, helped Morgan in his writing. Morgan told him that he had met a young woman who had a gift for words but lacked the consistency for hard graft that a true writer requires. Morgan said that he connected with her mind and 'thought waves', and the combination of her talent for wordiness with his doggedness helped him become a prolific writer.

O'Neill also claimed Morgan was aided by the spirit of a young man who had died before realising his dream of becoming a writer. Morgan was the spirit's tool, the pen for his voice. This cooperation with the astral plane explained, according to O'Neill, how Morgan knew the ingredients of a chemical substance that he needed for one of his stories. One day, Morgan, who knew nothing about chemistry, woke up from one of his naps with an entire formula in his mind. He wrote it down and had a chemistry professor check its validity. The professor verified it, and Morgan joked how he, a mere sailor, had been able to present a new formula to a chemistry professor. Did this astral connection help him write a story that foreshadowed the *Titanic* disaster? Aside from the similarities of the location of his *Titan*'s disaster, the month, the iceberg and too few lifeboats, there is also this to consider: *Titanic* was approximately 46,000 tonnes, 882 feet long and described as being 'practically unsinkable', while *Titan* was 45,000 tonnes, 800 feet in length and was given the exact same description, in the story, as being 'practically unsinkable'. Following the real sinking, in 1912, either Morgan or his publisher thought it necessary to change the tonnage of his fictional ship to 75,000 tonnes.

Desperate for money, Morgan went to a hypnotist to get suggestions for new work. The therapist felt that Morgan's brain was overworked from all the different stories he had written and regaled him about the great inventions of the world. O'Neill marvelled at the results after visiting Morgan one day and finding him mulling over an optics problem which ultimately resulted in the periscope that Morgan believed he had invented thanks to the hypnotherapy session.

Shortly before his death, he said, 'I am a sailor who has been transformed into a writer, inventor and several other things … but now I feel myself slipping back to the sea where I belong.' Is it overly fanciful to read between the lines that he knew his life was coming to an end and was signalling a return to where he had felt most at home?

12
· · ·

THE *TITANIC* TRAIL

LIVERPOOL

On Tuesday, 16 April 1912, the *Daily Sketch* newspaper printed three sentences about a peculiar incident that saw Liverpool plunged into darkness after her entire electrical supply failed. The blackout lasted forty-five minutes.

Liverpool is bound to the *Titanic* story, although the ship's scheduled visit to the city was cancelled at the last minute. However, Albion House, 30 James Street, Liverpool, was the headquarters of White Star Line, where Bruce Ismay had his office and from where marine superintendent Charles Bartlett supervised preparations for the epic maiden voyage. About ninety crew came from the Merseyside, including lookout Frederick Fleet and the six most senior engineers. It was the Liverpool firm CW and FN Black who supplied the musicians and, when they were lost, billed their relatives for their missing uniforms. Several Liverpool businesses were involved in the ship's construction. For example, Thomas Utley's firm designed the ship's bell and her 900 porthole windows while Stoniers supplied 50,000 bone china pieces. Captain Smith had lived in the city for forty years until 1908, his final address being 14 Marine Crescent in Waterloo, Liverpool, before he moved his family to Southampton. Today, *Titanic*'s Liverpool connections can be explored as part of the exhibition at the Merseyside Maritime Museum.

BELFAST

In 1912, Belfast was a busy city, a city where great plans found fruition. The population had multiplied from 25,000 inhabitants in 1808 to 385,000 in 1911. If you wanted a job, you came to Belfast; if you wanted to escape the uncertainty and vulnerability of rural life, you moved to Belfast. The city had established itself as a worldwide leader in linen production, while other flourishing industries included tobacco, rope-making, engineering and distilling. Yet perhaps the city's most enduring legacy, from the beginning of the twentieth century, was the ships she sent to sea because they included the biggest and most beautiful ships ever seen.

In 1854, Edward Harland arrived from England and got a position managing a shipyard in Queen's Island where he shook things up by demanding better work from the employees, whose wages he simultaneously cut. Five years later, he bought out the owner and, two years after that, acquired German Gustav Wolff as a business partner. After Harland's death in 1895, William James Pirrie became chairman while his nephew Thomas Andrews worked his way through the ranks. By 1900, the shipyard employed 9,000 people; albeit, no comparison to the numbers employed by the linen industry – approximately 30,000 – but eleven years later everyone would know the names, Harland and Wolff.

To date, the shipyard has received orders for 1,742 ships, with 93 cancellations and the orders have been for all sorts from a nine-ton ferry built in 1872 to HMS *Eagle*, in 1951, for the Royal Navy, one of the two largest aircraft carriers ever built.

Titanic was ready to leave Belfast on 1 April 1912, but a strong north-west wind that whipped the smoke from her three working funnels, delayed her departure until 6am the following morning. She would undertake twelve hours of sea trials before sailing to Southampton. While in Belfast, her captain had briefly been Herbert James Haddock from 25 March 1912, who inspected her crew and preparations, until he was relieved by Captain Smith on 31 March, thereby releasing him to take the helm of Smith's previous ship, *Olympic*. At sea, *Titanic* was put through her paces; exercises included making an emergency stop, wherein she took 850 yards to come to a halt, from a speed of 20 knots, along with a 40-mile cruise in the Irish Sea to judge her ability to maintain a lengthy straight line. Having passed all her tests under the watchful eye of Francis Carruthers, the Board of Trade inspector, she was now ready for service and returned to Belfast at approximately 6.30pm. The inspector signed her Board of Trade Certificate for Seaworthiness which was valid for one year. Presumably the ship's chart room was the location for the signing over of *Titanic* from Harland & Wolff shipyard to White Star Line. She was now a registered British steamship at the port of Liverpool, her official number 131,428. At 8pm, as her propellers whirled in readiness to sail to Southampton, nobody could ever have imagined that she was leaving Belfast behind forever.

SOUTHAMPTON

Titanic moored at Berth No. 44, White Star Dock, Southampton, just after midnight on 3 April 1912. It had taken no less than five Red Star tugs – *Ajax*, *Hector*, *Hercules*, *Neptune* and *Vulcan* – to manoeuvre her into place. She spent a week there, being fussed over by Thomas Andrews as he strove for perfection before her maiden voyage. He was the type of man who believed that if a thing was worth doing, then it was worth doing right and could be seen moving around chairs, tables and electric fans until they were just so.

Meanwhile, husbands, sweethearts, sons and brothers were bidding their families farewell, stepping out from their Southampton homes and boarding houses and heading to the docks to take up their new positions on *Titanic*. They would have considered themselves lucky to have a job. That April, a national coal strike resulted in 17,000 men out of work. White Star Line was pretty much the only company needing workers and over 500 Southampton residents joined up to work on *Titanic*'s maiden voyage: leading firemen, stokers, coal trimmers, greasers, engineers, electricians, telegraphists, barbers, clothes pressers, stewards, plumbers, able-bodied seamen, lookouts, store keepers, lamp trimmers, window cleaners, surgeons, postal clerks, bellboys, page boys, pursers, wine butlers, chefs, bakers, butchers, dishwashers and waiters, along with the female staff of twenty stewardesses and two restaurant cashiers.

Normally it is Addergoole, in County Mayo, that is named as having suffered the biggest percentage of loss of people from one area in April 1912, when 11 out of their group of 14 friends and neighbours were lost in the sinking. This is true in relation to passengers but there was a much, much bigger loss if you included the employees.

Out of 899 crew on *Titanic*, 724 had a Southampton address. A total of 686 crew died in the tragedy and 549 were from Southampton. It is hard to imagine the level of grief visited on the town. In one street in Northam, where a lot of the firemen and trimmers came from, every second house was left bereaved.

There is a story about a Southampton teacher asking her class to stand up if they had lost someone on *Titanic* and the entire class got to its feet. Eight men from Malmesbury Road went to work on *Titanic* and not one of them survived.

There are literally hundreds of pitiful stories to choose from amongst the women left widowed and the children fatherless. For example, Mrs Ann May, from 75 York Street, lost her husband, Arthur, and his namesake, their eldest son, Arthur. She had eight other children, the youngest being a year old. Living with her was her daughter-in-law, wife of Arthur (junior) who'd had a baby 12 weeks before *Titanic* went to sea. In an interview with the

Daily Sketch, published 18 April 1912, the family are waiting to hear if their loved ones had survived. Mrs May described how her husband and son planned to leave *Titanic* once they arrived back in Southampton. Her husband was tied to another ship that was temporarily grounded thanks to the coal strike.

Thirty-five-year-old Mrs Catherine Jane Wallis worked on the ship as a matron in second class. Mother of four children between the ages of three and twelve years, Mrs Wallis had lost her husband in January 1911 and then her father a few months after that. She was one of three female crew members who perished. Following her death, her children were split between relatives.

Shops closed, the flag at the town hall was flown at half-mast, blinds were drawn on public houses, children didn't turn up for school, and the mayor suspended a meeting of the Harbour Board. Southampton was in mourning.

As soon as the immense loss of life was confirmed there was an immediate recognition that most of the bereaved would need financial aid. Mothers with young children, suddenly bereft of the wage-earner, faced an uncertain future that could well involve the workhouse. The mayor of Southampton listed 227 widows and 363 now fatherless children under the age of fourteen years with 75 older children. Fortunately, there were campaigns under-way to help desperate families. One such was the S.O.S (Send on Shillings) Fund set up by the *Daily Sketch* newspaper on 19 April 1912. The idea behind it was that the readers were asked to send what they could, even if it was only a shilling. It got off to a great

DAILY SKETCH.

No. 973.—MONDAY, APRIL 22, 1912.   THE PREMIER PICTURE PAPER.   [Registered as a Newspaper.]   ONE HALFPENNY.

THE TRAGEDY PASSES BUT THE SORROW AND GRIEF REMAIN

The full story of the heroism and horror of the wreck of the Titanic is now fully known, but the sorrow and grief remain. To lighten the burden of the bereaved is the task of the nation, and all classes are responding to the call. How urgently monetary assistance is required the first photograph proves. Here is a family group over which the shadow of death hangs heavily. It represents the home circle at the house of Mrs. May, of 75, York-street, Southampton, who has suffered as great a bereavement as any one in the grief-stricken town. The mother of eight children—six of whom are seen in the photograph—she has lost her husband and also her eldest son, both firemen on the Titanic. On the extreme right is Mrs. May, junior, the widowed daughter-in-law of Mrs. May. In the young widow's arms is her twelve weeks' old baby, who will never know a father's care. It is for such and cases that the Daily Sketch appeals to you for help. On the wall is a portrait of the father, and inset is a picture of the son when a lad. The second picture shows a street in Northam, the district of Southampton where most of the Titanic's crew lived. Every other house contains bereaved families.—Daily Sketch Photographs.

Widow Mrs Ann May with her children, her widowed daughter-in-law start with the proprietors of the paper contributing 1,000 shillings. Then, on the 23 April, the paper felt obligated to berate its readers that had not yet sent in their shilling. They reckoned that one million read the paper every morning, but the fund had received far less than a million shillings. Southampton Football Club, which was set up in 1885, cancelled a much-needed funding drive for the club. One assumes that its supporters included many of the dead – for instance, lookout Frederick Fleet was supposedly a fan. Over in Windsor Park, in Belfast, Linfield played against Blackburn in front of 5,000 spectators and the money, £173, went to the *Titanic* relief fund. It was the first of several matches played in aid of the *Titanic* fund. On 6 May, the *Exeter and Plymouth Gazette*, who set up their own campaign, wrote that the football season had been especially extended so that more money could be raised for the *Titanic* relatives.

Meanwhile, another article reported that the Mansion House *Titanic* Fund had already reached £100,000 thanks to the likes of the Marquis of Salisbury who contributed £100. Wives and children of the Southampton crew would benefit from the money raised. White Star Line also made payments of compensation for the loss of the victims. The amounts ranged from £300 for a steward, £294 for a leading firemen and greaser, £237 for a fireman and £223 for a trimmer.

Ninety survivors arrived back in Southampton on 29 April and the *Daily Sketch* was there to bear witness to the emotional scenes as the lucky families and friends were reunited. For the bereaved families, there was the added shock that their loved ones were lost forevermore. No bodies arrived back in Southampton for burial. Even if a body had been identified and had not been returned to the Atlantic, the families of the crew could not afford to bring their relatives home. There are 60 *Titanic*-related headstones, the names include Mrs Catherine Jane Wallis and the two Arthur Mays, father and son, in Southampton Old Cemetery but none lie in the ground.

Today, there are several *Titanic* memorials in Southampton, including the Millvina Dean Memorial Garden, a tribute to the last survivor who boarded *Titanic* at nine weeks of age, the youngest passenger, and died on 31 May 2009, in a Southampton nursing home, at the grand old age of ninety-seven.

On Wednesday 10 April, as *Titanic* left Southampton, she almost collided with the American liner, the *New York*, after the latter's ropes snapped in the turbulence caused by the biggest ship in the world and she was sucked into *Titanic's* path. Fortunately, *Titanic's* propellers were stalled in the nick of time but it meant her journey would be delayed by an hour or so.

After the tragedy, some people would think upon this near miss as being a sinister omen.

CHERBOURG

Having left Southampton an hour later than planned, *Titanic* finally reached Cherbourg in France, the biggest artificial harbour in the world, at 6.35pm local time and stayed for approximately ninety minutes. Twenty-two fortunate passengers disembarked here, while approximately 271 got on, ferried out to *Titanic* by the two White Star tenders, SS *Nomadic*, who took the first and second-class passengers, and SS *Traffic* who carried the 102 third-class passengers. A mere twenty-one passengers were French – of whom sixteen would survive, while the rest were from America, Syria, Russia, Lebanon, Italy, Britain, Canada, Belgium, Poland and Uruguay. First-class passengers on the SS *Nomadic* included the American Margaret Brown and John Jacob Astor. Victuals were also loaded onto *Titanic*, including 75 pounds of meat, 10,000 bottles of wine, 15,000 bottles of beer and 12,000 bottles of mineral water. Once all were safely on board, along with luggage and mail, *Titanic* set out for her final scheduled stop at Queenstown, Ireland, and she must have made quite a sight as it was dusk and, so, her lights were lit.

QUEENSTOWN (COBH)

It was here that Father Browne received his Provincial's telegram in answer to his request to be allowed to travel to New York, at the behest of a rich American couple, who offered to pay his fare, 'Get off that ship.'

Originally called Cove (today the town is spelled Cobh), this harbour town was renamed Queenstown in 1849 in honour of a visit by Queen Victoria, even though Her Majesty barely stepped down onto Cove soil before taking her leave again.

Queenstown was the final stop for *Titanic* on her way to America and, ultimately, the last time she would be seen from land. She arrived after midday on Thursday 11 April and stayed for two hours, two miles off shore, at Roches Point, because the harbour was too small for her to turn. Therefore, the 123 waiting passengers were obliged to queue up at the White Star Line pier to board the two tenders, PS (paddle-wheel steamship) *Ireland* and PS *America*, who would ferry them out to *Titanic* after the bags of mail had been collected at Deepwater Quay. Three were for first class, seven went into second class, while the rest were steerage/third class. Local vendors accompanied these passengers in the tenders, to hastily construct pop-up stalls and sell their wares on *Titanic's*

White Star Line passengers in Queenstown (Cobh), waiting to be ferried out to *Titanic*.

deck. Colonel John Jacob Astor spent £165 on a lace shawl for his wife. At 1.30 in the afternoon, a blasting of whistles between *Titanic* and the two tenders, signified that all was on board and she was ready to leave for New York.

It must have been an emotional scene as very few of the new steerage passengers hardly expected to see Ireland and their extended families again. They were embarking on a bold adventure, having saved every penny towards a new home and life in America.

One of these passengers was nineteen-year-old Jeremiah Burke, from Glanmire, Cork, who was travelling with his cousin Nora Hegarty. At some point, Jeremiah wrote a message in pencil, stuck it in a bottle and flung it from *Titanic*. Remarkably, a year later, the bottle, with its message, was found by a man walking his dog at Cork Harbour. Neither Jeremiah nor Nora survived the sinking and their bodies were never found. How peculiar then for his relatives to read what must have felt like a prophetic note, '*From Titanic, Goodbye All, Burke of Glanmire*'. There is a theory that he might have thrown it into the water when he knew all was lost. According to family, the bottle had contained holy water, given to him by his mother; and anyone with any amount of Irish blood running through their veins would struggle to believe that a son would empty out his mother's holy water for fun. Today, the original note forms part of the *Titanic* exhibition in Cobh's Heritage Centre.

The actual White Star pier that the passengers waited on is still there today. Only 44 of the 271 survived the sinking.

Thanks to two native Cork photographers, *Titanic's* stop off at Queenstown is well documented. Jesuit priest, Father Frank Browne was leaving the ship after his two-day trip aboard, spent meeting crew and passengers and taking their photographs. The tenders, PS *Ireland* and PS *America*, brought out fresh passengers and the press, including *Cork Examiner* photographer Tom Baker. He took the only photograph in existence of steerage passengers who were taking the first steps of their journey to a new life, having just left the pier, that is, Cork soil, and are pictured standing together in the *America* waiting to be ferried out to the biggest ship in the world.

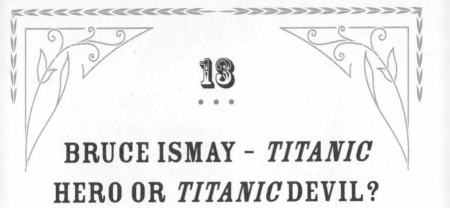

BRUCE ISMAY - *TITANIC* HERO OR *TITANIC* DEVIL?

The following took place on Tuesday, 30 April, during the 1912 Senate investigation of the sinking:

Senator Smith: 'Who, if anyone, told you to enter that lifeboat (Collapsible C)?'

Bruce Ismay: 'No one, sir.'

Senator Smith: 'Why did you enter it?'

Bruce Ismay: 'Because there was room in the boat. She was being lowered away. I felt the ship was going down and I got into the boat …'

When the seventy-four-year-old Joseph Bruce Ismay died on 17 October 1937, in London, *The Times* obituary made no mention of *Titanic*, concentrating, instead, on his merits, his shyness and sensitivity along with his inclination for caring about the vulnerable. His sporting capabilities were also highlighted; he had won prizes for tennis and played football before excelling as a keen hunter and fisherman, the latter he enjoyed doing in Connemara, Ireland.

Bruce Ismay, director of White Star Line
and infamous survivor of the sinking.

Meanwhile, the title of the obituary in *The Washington Post* was stark, to say the least, 'Owner who fled stricken *Titanic* dies as recluse', while *The New York Times* concentrated only on Ismay's *Titanic* connection.

Essentially, when the opportunity arose, Bruce Ismay chose to save himself after spending the previous sixty minutes or so helping to load lifeboats. His eagerness to help had incurred the wrath of Fifth Officer Lowe who shouted at him to get out of his way. Maybe Ismay had never considered his role on board if disaster befell any of his ships. Walter Lord described him as bouncing between being a passenger enjoying the first-class luxuries provided by *Titanic* to acting the part of a 'super-captain' who, allegedly, decided, in Queenstown, the ship's speed for the journey. As *Titanic* is sinking, he is crew, helping women and children into the boats, including Australian stewardess Evelyn Marsden who was unsure if she was, as a member of staff, entitled to a space until Ismay directed her into Lifeboat 16, telling her and her colleagues, 'You are all women now.'

Finally, as if taking his own advice to Miss Marsden, he becomes a passenger once more and jumps into Collapsible C, the last boat to be launched from the forward starboard side. There had been repeated calls for more women and children but none answered. People were presumably moving backwards, away from the ocean that was wilfully dragging *Titanic*'s bow below sea level and, consequently, there were no women and children left in shouting distance.

Meanwhile, Bruce Ismay had five children, three sons and two daughters, plus a loving wife waiting for him at home. One can easily imagine a would-be survivor, at that moment, understanding only two things, firstly that it was imperative to get into a lifeboat and secondly there was no time to debate the first thing. Ismay was one of a few men who jumped in. Under Officers Wilde and Murdoch's supervision, the collapsible, carrying approximately forty-four passengers, reached the water at about 2am. Twenty minutes later, Ismay kept his back firmly to the sight of *Titanic's* submersion into the Atlantic.

Not surprisingly, he had a tough time during both the American and the British hearings. During the latter, Mr Ismay pleaded ignorance regarding navigational matters, referring to himself as an 'ordinary passenger'. However, Lord Mersey, the High Court judge who was overseeing the inquiry, dismantled this description with one question, 'Did you pay your fare?' No ordinary passenger was sailing for free on *Titanic*, ergo Bruce Ismay was no ordinary passenger.

It was not simply that he had jumped into Collapsible C, there was also the matter of the iceberg warning that Captain Smith had received from the *Baltic* on Sunday afternoon. He gave it to Mr Ismay who said that he stuck it in his pocket and forgot about it for five hours or so. Yet, first-class passenger Mrs Emily Ryerson claimed that Bruce Ismay had showed her the telegram, in fact she said he handed it to her, telling her they were now amongst the icebergs. She could not remember much of what the telegram contained, but she did remember Ismay telling her that *Titanic* was presently only travelling at 20 or 21 knots and, therefore, extra boilers were to be lit that very evening to, Mrs Ryerson assumed, increase the ship's speed. She could not say that the White Star director used the word 'record' but generally felt he wanted to surprise everybody with their arrival time in New York. In any case, Mr Ismay made it clear that there was no time to go to the assistance of the SS *Deutchland*, which was, according to the rest of the telegram, out of coal and needed help. Mrs Ryerson retained the impression that no time could be spared to stop and tow the German ship into New York's harbour. Mrs Ryerson also said that she did not want to talk to Mr Ismay and was just, out of politeness, playing her part in the conversation. Her reluctance for small talk was understandable as the reason she and her family – husband Arthur, son John, daughters Suzette and Emily – were on *Titanic* was that they were travelling back to America for the funeral of her eldest son, Arthur, who had died in a car crash on Easter Monday, 8 April 1912.

When asked about this conversation for his American deposition, Mr Ismay needed prompting to agree to Mrs Ryerson's presence after he initially only remembered talking to Mrs Thayer. He admitted to holding up the telegram in front of the women and that he read aloud the part that referred to icebergs and the *Deutchland*. Furthermore, he said the broken-down steamer distracted him from the notion of icebergs.

Back in Britain, Lord Mersey asked about the conversation that related to the icebergs and *Titanic*'s speed. When she heard about the ice, Mrs Ryerson asked would the ship be slowed, to which she received the reply, 'No, we will put on more boilers to get out of it.' When these words were put to Bruce Ismay by Lord Mersey, he rejected having said them with an emphatic, 'Certainly not'.

On Sunday, 21 April 1912, the *Washington Herald* published an article about Canadian Major Arthur Peuchen laying the blame for the tragedy on Ismay's disregard for icebergs. He was supported in this by first-class passenger Mrs Mahala Douglas. They were standing next to one another on *Carpathia* when Mrs Ryerson described how a few hours before the collision she had asked Mr Ismay if the ship would be slowed down because of icebergs, to which she said he replied, 'On the contrary, we are going to go along faster than we have been going.'

It is worth noting that Mrs Ryerson chose not to swear about her encounters with Bruce Ismay in her affidavit for the US Senate Investigation. Perhaps she had not the heart to add to his troubles or to be instrumental in his downfall. It is hard to grasp the extent of her grief, returning home for her eldest son's funeral and having to postpone it after losing her husband to *Titanic*. In fact, Mr Ryerson's last act was to save their youngest son, thirteen-year-old John, by demanding that he be allowed into a lifeboat after a crewman refused to have him.

During the British inquiry, Mr Ismay was repeatedly asked about the fact that Captain Smith had given him the telegram in the first place and time was spent deliberating when this had happened.

Mr Ismay had been unsure about the timing in America but now remembered that he had read and pocketed the 'marconigram' before lunch on Sunday afternoon. It was accepted that the captain would have received several telegrams by then yet this was the only one he handed to the director who gave it but his briefest attention. When asked once more about Mrs Ryerson, Mr Ismay thought that he could pledge, or promise, that she had never asked him about slowing the ship. Following that, there was some discussion about *Titanic's* speed which led to Mr Ismay's conversation with *Titanic's* Chief Engineer Joseph Bell, on Thursday, 11 April, at Queenstown (Cobh), when they decided that – weather permitting – *Titanic* would be pushed to her maximum speed for a few hours on either Monday or Tuesday.

An agreement was reached by Mr Ismay and his interrogators that *Titanic's* speed was not reduced after he read the telegram. He admits that he knew the ship was approaching the ice, although he was not sure where it was in relation to *Titanic* since he did not understand longitude or latitude. One can imagine a gasp as Mr Ismay was asked to reconsider what he, a managing director of a shipping line, had just admitted. The director rushed to say that all he meant was that the telegram did not convey to him where exactly the ice was. At any rate, any change in the ship's route, to avoid ice or otherwise, had nothing to do with him as navigational duties rested solely with Captain Smith. A tense moment unfolded when Mr Ismay was pointedly asked if it was not desirable for a ship to slow down, at night, in an area containing icebergs. Mr

Ismay refused to answer on the basis that he was not a navigator. Lord Mersey ordered him to answer the question and again he refused, resulting in a reprimand from the attorney general (Sir Rufus Isaacs) about his lack of honesty. Sir Robert Finlay, leading counsel for the White Star Line, immediately protested this. Mr Ismay was obliged to admit that he did not see any need to reduce speed if a man could see that the way ahead was free of all obstacles and this was why he did not expect Captain Smith to slacken the ship's speed.

Later in the proceedings, Thomas Scanlan, representing the National Sailors' and Firemen's Union, asked Mr Ismay what right he had to decide the ship's speed without consulting the ship's captain. Lord Mersey jumped in and answered the question, that Mr Ismay had no right at all. It is then that we hear mention of the description 'super captain' with Scanlan's definition that a super captain is a man who can tell the ship's engineer what speed the ship is to make. His tone may have been sarcastic.

Ultimately, Bruce Ismay was cleared of any wrongdoing. On 26 June 1912, the *Daily Sketch* published Sir Robert Farley's belief that Bruce Ismay's remaining aboard the sinking ship would not have saved another life. Furthermore, that had the managing director gone down with the ship, his critics would have accused him of having done so purely to avoid inquiry. As an argument, or explanation, it is not overly convincing.

Yet, it raises an interesting point, how much courage did it take for Bruce Ismay to save himself? In his second appearance before the US investigators, the most senior officer to survive, Second Officer Charles Lightoller, testified that the White Star director was in a terrible state on *Carpathia*, lamenting the fact he had survived when women had died. As a matter of fact, according to Lightoller, Ismay had no choice in the matter, having been bundled into the lifeboat by Officer Wilde, whom he described as physically big and powerful. Lightoller emphasised that there were no women or children to be seen. One can make the argument that Lightoller was a company man and doing his best to help his boss as it is peculiar that he only remembers Wilde forcing Mr Ismay into the collapsible on his second appearance. Equally, one can make the argument that Bruce Ismay needed some defence in front of the Americans, considering how soon after the disaster the inquiry took place. And might not it be a factor that the Americans were under more pressure to lay blame since the most important, that is, the richest and most famous victims of the sinking were their fellow patriots?

Alfred Stead, whose brother, journalist William Stead, numbered amongst the British victims, agreed with America's indignation and was reported in the 20 April 1912 edition of the American *Providence Journal*, asking what right Bruce Ismay had to be saved over so many others whose lives were the responsibility of White Star Line.

Bruce Ismay kept to himself on *Carpathia*, which is understandable. Whatever he did or did not do, he would have been racked with regret, fear and sorrow. What could he possibly have said to the other survivors, to those women who had lost husbands and sons? Who has the words for that sort of conversation? One first-class widow, the teenage Mrs Eloise Smith, complained about the White Star director having the best cabin to himself while so many others were forced to sleep on the floor due to the shortage of space. The *Washington Post* mistakenly reported that Mr Ismay had been helped by a group of crewmen into one of the first lifeboats to leave *Titanic*, basing their report on the claims of Mrs Smith, the young wife who told of pleading with Captain Smith in vain to allow her husband to accompany her into a lifeboat. Emotions were running high and understandably so.

In America, Senator Alden Smith summed up his findings in the wake of his investigation. Regarding Bruce Ismay, Senator Smith found him innocent of urging Captain Smith to go faster but qualified that by saying he believed that the presence of the White Star Managing Director may have influenced the captain into sailing faster than he should have.

On 28 June 1912, the *Daily Sketch* reported on Lord Mersey and Sir Rufus Isaacs's findings, that Bruce Ismay did not interfere with the ship's navigation and that no speed record had been ventured regarding *Titanic*'s arrival time in New York.

A month after the sinking, on 15 May 1912, *The New York Times* reported that Mr and Mrs Ismay offered $55,000 to the mayor of Liverpool to be made available as pensions for wives whose husbands had been lost at sea whilst working on British ships – this was to include the widows of *Titanic*'s crew. Mr Ismay also provided financial assistance to the family of his secretary, William Henry Harrison, who had not survived the sinking.

Walter Lord wrote in *The Night Lives On* that Ismay had been planning to retire from his White Star role before the tragedy but then, following 15 April, he felt obliged to stay on as he did not want to look like he was running away out of guilt or shame. His American bosses, however, did not want him, or his now shabby reputation, associated with the shipping company, and he did finally retire on 30 June 1913.

Writers and historians argue over the use of the word 'recluse' to describe his position after this. In fact, he continued working for The Liverpool and London Steamship Protection and Indemnity Association Limited and oversaw thousands of pounds of compensation being paid out to the relatives of *Titanic* victims. He inaugurated the *Mersey*, a training ship for British navy cadets, and donated £11,000 to enable a fund to be set up in aid of families who lost a naval relative at sea. In 1919, he used £25,000 to set up a fund that marked the contribution made by merchant mariners during the First World War. It seems that he spent the rest of his life giving back to those who he may have felt obligated to.

14

. . .

ERNEST SHACKLETON
AND *TITANIC*

ight months after *Titanic* sank into the Atlantic Ocean, a
Norwegian ship, reputed to be the strongest wooden ship
ever built, was completed and launched. Her name was *Endurance*.
Her life span would be two years and eleven months and, like
Titanic, her brutal end would be the result of ice, although *Endurance*'s demise would be less dramatic as the frozen waters of the
Weddell Sea slowly shattered her in front of her appalled crew and
their captain, Ernest Shackleton.

By 1912, Irishman Ernest Shackleton was already a celebrated
explorer. King Edward VII had both raised him to Commander of
the Royal Victorian Order (CVO) and made him a knight. And,
in June 1912, Sir Ernest Shackleton was asked to take part in the
British Wreck Commissioner's Inquiry into the sinking of *Titanic*
to provide an expert opinion about icebergs.

When asked how far a dark iceberg could be seen on a clear
night, Sir Ernest replied that a berg might be seen three miles off
but would be difficult to spot if you are looking down from a

Polar explorer, Sir Ernest Shackleton whose expert opinion was ultimately disregarded by the British Inquiry.

height. It would be much easier to detect a berg if it were taller than the observer. A discussion ensued on where best to situate crew to look for icebergs since it seems that Sir Ernest did not have much faith in the crow's nest. He believed that it would be best to be as near to the waterline as possible and that the best method was two lookouts, one in the crow's nest and one down on deck.

But what if, he was asked, he only had the use of the crow's nest and the ship had entered dangerous waters. Sir Ernest answered honestly that, in that case, he would reduce the ship's speed. When he was asked what he would do with a ship travelling at 21 to 22 knots in an ice region, his reply was blunt, 'You have no right to go at that speed in an ice region.'

Was Sir Ernest criticising Captain Smith's judgement, ten days after Bruce Ismay's first appearance at the inquiry?

Again, the explorer was asked about lookouts and he repeated his belief that it was necessary, in an ice region, to have one man in the crow's nest and a second on deck, near the water. It is easy to imagine heads nodding in agreement as he declared that a man working alone would be naturally more vigilant than two men standing side by side.

On being asked about eye-glasses, or binoculars, he said he did not believe in lookouts having them as their eyes were enough to spot an obstacle in time to bring it to the attention of an officer who can then verify it with his binoculars. Next, he was asked whether a fall in temperature signalled that icebergs were nearby.

Sir Ernest replied that it would depend if there was wind or not. If there is no wind, then, yes, a sudden drop in temperature was a clear warning about the possibility of ice in the water. The attorney general related that, on the afternoon of 14 April, the drop in temperature was so drastic that Captain Smith asked the carpenter to check against water freezing in his tanks and, thus, Sir Ernest was obliged to admit that the freezing temperature and calm sea clearly indicated that icebergs were in *Titanic's* vicinity. The calmness of the ocean, as reported by Officer Lightoller, was remarked upon for its rarity. The danger was the silence of a dead calm sea, lacking a swell, where there would be no breaking, or splashing, of water against an iceberg.

The topic of speed was raised again, and Sir Ernest described how his old ship, whose top speed was only six knots, was reduced to four knots on entering an ice region. When asked about the speed of liners and *Titanic*, he declared himself unqualified to talk about liners but allowed that perhaps a liner should travel at only ten knots in an ice area – particularly at night – until they have passed the problem spot. It is a reasonable response but not one that would sit well with shipping companies.

Next, he was asked if the practice of ships travelling through the North Atlantic, over the last thirty years, was incorrect. It was a big question. Sir Ernest attempted to clarify his opinion by not agreeing that the usual practice was wrong, just that the current situation was a result of a long-developed habit to satisfy the desires of the public for speed as well as dealing with competition.

He believed that experienced seamen were under orders from the owners of the shipping companies. Did this influence Lord Mersey's findings when he wrote in his final report that Captain Smith may have been influenced by the presence onboard of White Star Line Managing Director Bruce Ismay?

In a further discussion about speed, Sir Ernest was asked if it was necessary to reduce speed if icebergs were clearly seen in time to avoid them. No was his answer; however, he qualified that by doubting that icebergs would be detected in time to steer clear of them. The berg in this case was reputed to be dark, making detection even more difficult on a calm sea. Sir Ernest agreed it would be hard to see this iceberg, particularly, from 'a ship going at that speed'. He estimated that the berg might have been just three quarters of a mile from *Titanic* before it was spotted. In the face of incredulity from his interviewers, he declared that it was both a possibility and a probability for the iceberg not to have been spotted in time by three pairs of eyes, the two lookouts and the officer on the bridge of *Titanic*. The term 'abnormal' is used repeatedly to describe that night of the flat sea and black iceberg.

He was then asked a controversial question. Did Sir Ernest believe that a good lookout was kept that night? He answers in the affirmative but added that it was an advantage to have just one man in the crow's nest as men standing next to one another sometimes chat, something Sir Ernest remembered doing in his early days.

Next, he was asked a delicate question about Captain Smith, if he had been justified, as someone who had been in the business for twenty-five years, in following the usual practice of crossing the ocean at top speed despite the danger of icebergs? Sir Ernest described it as natural for the captain to do the 'usual' thing but that, thanks to the advent of wirelesses, any accident could be avoided now.

Sir Ernest may have wondered if his appearance had been a waste of his time when the representative for White Star Line, Sir Robert Finlay, criticised his testimony about Atlantic captains travelling through the Atlantic at full speed because they have been instructed to do by the owners of the shipping companies. Sir Robert Finlay felt that this theory proved the explorer's 'complete ignorance' of the North Atlantic trade. Sir Ernest is supreme regarding the South Pole, allowed Sir Robert, but in the North Atlantic he is but 'an ordinary man' because, of course, a captain wants to be thought efficient and capable by his employer but not enough to take risks with their ship and passengers.

15
. . .

THE SS *CALIFORNIAN* AND
THE 'MYSTERY SHIP'

*T*itanic's sinking was a stark reminder of man's inferiority to nature and the ultimate lack of control he has over his fate. It seemed too incredible, that this magnificent vessel, recently celebrated in news reels and newspapers, was sunk by an iceberg on her maiden voyage. How could the likes of John Jacob Astor be dead? Naturally, when it emerged that there had been another ship nearby, a British one, whose captain and officers had ignored *Titanic*'s white rockets of distress, a witch hunt ensued.

Thirty-five-year-old Stanley Lord was the captain on the Scottish-built SS *Californian*, primarily a cargo ship with room for forty-seven passengers. On 5 April 1912, she left Liverpool, with just crew on board, on her way to Boston, Massachusetts. Cyril Evans was her only wireless operator. Captain Lord's Second and Third officers were Herbert Stone and Charles Grove, and James Gibson was the young apprentice.

As night fell on 14 April 1912, Captain Lord doubled the lookout on the SS *Californian*, putting one man on deck, at the front of the ship, while he joined an officer at the bridge. Furthermore, at 10.21pm when it became apparent that there was ice about, the captain had the ship stalled for the night, deciding it was too dangerous to continue. It is hard not to compare this cautious behaviour with that of Captain Smith.

To this day, a question over the SS *Californian* divides *Titanic* enthusiasts – could the *Californian* have saved lives? Her captain and officers were interrogated during both the American and the British inquiries. Newspapers at the time decided who was to blame for the tragic loss of life, scapegoating *Californian*'s Captain Stanley Lord and his crew for not coming to the aid of *Titanic* as over 1,500 souls perished. One

Stanley Lord, the strict disciplinarian who captained the SS *Californian*.

of the key issues is just how far away from the sinking *Titanic* was the *Californian*? Captain Lord testified to being between nineteen and a half to twenty miles away, but this was controversial considering that the lights of a ship were visible to himself and his officers. Charles Grove said he could make out two mast lines. Furthermore, several white rockets were clearly seen by Second Officer Herbert Stone and the apprentice, James Gibson, who chatted about what they were looking at, agreeing that no ship fires rockets for nothing. The last one, rocket number eight, was seen at 1.40am and then it seemed to Stone that the ship steamed away, her lights disappearing bit by bit.

Meanwhile, the wireless operator was left to sleep until 3.30am, while Captain Lord appeared to sleep soundly, although Stone contacted him on the voice tube about the ship and her white rockets and then, when it seemed she disappeared, sent the apprentice Gibson down to tell the captain in person. Captain Lord had told his Second Officer to keep an eye on the ship and let him know of any developments. He had also ordered Stone to communicate with the ship using the Morse lamp, but this produced no results.

Afterwards, there were major discrepancies between the captain's version and that of his Second Officer. Captain Lord, who had spied the ship himself, starboard side, about six or seven miles away, as early as 11pm, had no recollection of these two conversations, only remembering Gibson opening and closing his door. An absence of blazing lights convinced the captain that it was a much smaller ship than *Titanic*, that it was a medium-sized steamer like his own.

One particularly sad detail was that Cyril Evans contacted the ship at approximately 11.05pm, on behalf of Captain Lord, to tell her that the *Californian* was surrounded by ice and therefore stopping for the night. Evans was told to 'Shut Up!' by *Titanic*'s Marconi operator, Jack Phillips, because he was busy. Evans listened to *Titanic*'s signals for a while before taking off his headphones at 11.35pm, five minutes before *Titanic* hit the iceberg.

When the lifeboats were being loaded on *Titanic*, sailors were told to make for the lights in the distance. Some of *Titanic*'s crew, including Captain Smith, believed they could see another ship. Survivors spoke of rowing towards the lights but never reaching them.

Finally, Cyril Evans was awakened at 5.30am, thanks to Chief Officer Stewart, who had recently come on watch and heard about the ship and her rockets; how bewildering is it that he was the only one to think of asking the radio man to check it out. Within five minutes of switching on his machine, Evans is told by the *Virginian* that *Titanic* has sank. At 6am, Captain Lord set his course for *Titanic*'s last position, and the *Californian* was steered carefully through the thickest ice, which took thirty minutes, and then, once clear of the worst, she went at full speed, arriving at *Carpathia*'s side at 8.30am, to help in the search for survivors.

The final report made by the 1912 Senate investigating committee concluded that the *Californian* was closer to *Titanic* than

Captain Lord's stated nineteen and a half to twenty miles and deemed it reprehensible that the crew failed to respond to the rockets, an obvious sign of a ship in distress. It placed a 'grave responsibility' on Captain Stanley Lord.

The final report by the British Wreck Commissioners Inquiry stated that the *Californian* was between five and eight miles, or ten miles maximum, away from *Titanic* and on sighting the first white rocket, the ship should have pushed through the ice and consequently would have saved many or even all those lives which were lost.

In 1956, following the publication of bestselling *A Night To Remember*, in which Walter Lord upheld the *Californian's* failure to charge to *Titanic's* aid, no doubt influenced by his correspondence with Third Officer Charles Grove, who was no fan of his *Californian* colleagues, seventy-nine-year-old Stanley Lord wanted the case reopened to clear his name of any wrongdoing. However, no one was interested until 1992, eighty years after the tragedy, when the Marine Accident branch launched a fresh investigation into the *Californian's* role that night. Of course, by 1992, *Titanic's* wreck had been discovered by Doctor Robert Ballard, thirteen miles from where they thought it was in 1912. Therefore, the 1992 investigator reported that the *Californian* was actually eighteen miles away from *Titanic*. He also writes that since no one on *Titanic* saw another ship until after the collision there must have been a third ship in the area and this was the 'mystery' ship that was seen by the crew on the *Californian* and the *Titanic*.

After the tragedy, Henrik Naess, from the Norwegian sealer ship, the *Samson*, claimed to have seen *Titanic*'s lights that night and the *Samson* was believed to be the third ship. The crew were illegally hunting seals and, on seeing rockets, thought that a US coast guard vessel was in pursuit so they left as fast as they could.

In any case, both the 1912 inquiries and the 1992 Marine Accident investigators agreed that *Titanic*'s rockets were seen by the crew on the *Californian* and, although, it was later shown that the *Samson* was nowhere near *Titanic*, the point is made that rockets could be used for different reasons.

Ultimately, Second Officer Herbert Stone, the 1992 investigator recorded, ought to have done a lot more than he did. Flashing a Morse lamp was an inadequate response to sighting rockets. He should have presented himself in person to Captain Lord, ensuring that the captain fully appreciated the situation, and once he had done that, Officer Stone should have put the engine room on standby before summoning Cyril Evans from his bed back to his radio. Captain Lord should have gone to the bridge, checked that the engine room was ready and that Cyril Evans was at his post and then should have directed his ship towards the source of the rockets.

Regarding Captain Lord's claim not to remember a conversation with Herbert Stone, through the voice tube, nor a second one with apprentice James Gibson, who had stood in front of him, about the colour of the rockets, the 1992 report considers that the captain was in a state of 'somnambulism', more asleep

TWENTY-FOUR-YEAR-OLD HERBERT STONE WAS SERIOUSLY AT FAULT FOR NOT GOING TO THE CAPTAIN IN PERSON.

than awake, and never actually came to full consciousness. Twenty-four-year-old Herbert Stone was seriously at fault for not going to the captain in person. He may have feared to leave the bridge, normally treated as a gross negligence of duty, and he may have feared Captain Lord himself, who was known to be a humourless disciplinarian. The report sympathises with Stone and feels that the young man just wanted it not to be true, that something was seriously wrong, so he continued standing there, counting rockets, and – presumably – ignoring his instinct.

A valid point is also raised about the colour of the rockets. Back in 1912, rockets signalling a ship's distress could be any colour and it wasn't until 1948 that it was decided that distress would be signalled by red rockets. If there had been a specific colour in 1912, then the tentative Herbert Stone would have surely reacted to what he understood to be a definite cry for help. The investigator writes that there were no villains here, only flawed human beings.

In any case, the report concluded that had the *Californian* started towards *Titanic*, as soon as the first rocket was sighted, she might have only arrived in time to see the ship sink and, therefore, would not have saved any more lives than those already in the lifeboats.

Afterwards, only Herbert Stone paid the price for the *Californian*'s inaction. Judged unfit to ever command a ship, he left the navy, tormented by guilt, to become a dock labourer, dying in poverty. The rest of the crew, Stanley Lord, apprentice James Gibson and Third Officer Charles Groves continued with their naval careers, Captain Charles Groves going on to serve with distinction in both world wars.

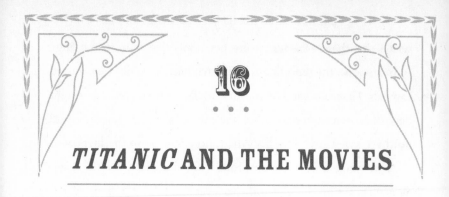

16
. . .

TITANIC AND THE MOVIES

SAVED FROM THE TITANIC (1912)

Actress and model, Dorothy Winifred Gibson (1889–1946), was travelling with her mother Pauline and they were lucky to be able to get into Lifeboat 7.

Largely forgotten today, Gibson was responsible for the first *Titanic* movie, which came out on 16 May, a mere month after the sinking. Apparently, she wore the same dress and shoes in the film that she had worn on 14 and 15 April. About fifteen minutes in duration, *Saved from the Titanic* received great reviews, while others vowed to ignore it, deploring the act of using such a devastating – and too recent tragedy – for a commercial product. Unfortunately, the film was lost in a studio fire. However, on YouTube, there is a ten-minute reel by the same name that brings Captain Smith and a host of, it must be said, rather jovial-looking individuals to life. The ship in the footage is probably *Olympic* while the blessed *Carpathia* plays a starring role.

Dorothy acted in silent shorts – one-reelers – twenty-five in all; eighteen were made in 1912 alone. In fact, she was one of the

The last publicity photo of actress Dorothy
Gibson, whose 1912 film, *Saved from the Titanic*,
was the first of its kind.

highest paid actresses at the time which possibly explains why and how she retired from acting in May 1912 to pursue a singing career.

Married three times, her last husband was movie mogul Jules Brulatour who took six years to leave his wife for her. Historian Randy Bryan Bigham, in his biography, *Finding Dorothy*, suggests that it was Brulatour's instigation, in sensing the perfect business venture regarding marketing and publicity, that pushed her to make the film mere weeks after her rescue. According to the film crew, she broke down on set as she was, presumably, still in shock. They married in 1917 but it hardly lasted two years when Brulatour lost his heart to another, younger actress. To escape the gossip and her broken heart, Dorothy left America with her mother to live in Paris. During the Second World War, she was a suspected Nazi sympathiser and was even accused of spying for the Germans, though this was never proved. Undergoing a complete change of heart, she renounced Nazism. She was arrested by the Gestapo in Italy for being a resistance agitator and was subsequently jailed in the notorious San Vittore in Milan, but managed to escape in 1944 with two other prisoners, journalist Indro Montanelli and General Bartolo Zambon.

She died at home, that is, her room in the Ritz Hotel in Paris, from a heart attack.

TITANIC (1943)

The sinking of *Titanic* was used by the Nazis to make a point about British and American greed. Joseph Goebbels chose the director himself, Herbert Selpin, but then had him arrested and killed for criticising the boorish behaviour of Nazi officers on set. The rest of the cast and crew were warned that anyone who avoided the man who reported the director would answer to Goebbels himself. Most of the film was shot on the SS *Cap Arcona*, the liner that was ultimately used to hide approximately 5,500 survivors from concentration camps and was left out in the open with the hope that it would be sunk by the allies, which it was, on 3 May 1945, with a huge loss of life.

In the film, the British first-class passengers are cowards, while any German character is brave and good, including the main hero, the German First Officer who, amongst other things, rescues a child who has been stranded by her callous parents. Furthermore, Bruce Ismay's priority is raising the White Star Line stock on the market and, at the film's close, 1,500 are dead thanks to capitalist Britain's love of profit.

Four clips of the ship in this Nazi film were used in the 1958 British film, *A Night to Remember*.

On its release, Goebbels decided that the film *Titanic*, which had spiralled wildly over budget, was not in the best interest of the German nation and banned it. His attitude possibly resulted from the emotional scenes depicting steerage passengers talking through bars of locked gates, desperately searching for their relatives, which proved too similar to what was happening in the concentration camps and might accidentally spark a misplaced compassion for foreigners in a German audience.

TITANIC (1953)

Winner of the 1953 Oscar for Best Original Screenplay, it was also nominated for Best Art Direction, this film stars Barbara Stanwyck and Clifton Webb who play an estranged husband and wife on *Titanic*, whose bitter war is eclipsed by the ship's fatal collision with an iceberg. Stanwyck experienced genuine emotion during the sinking segment when, from her lifeboat, she looked at the extras on the fictional ship with sudden clarity over what the real passengers went through in April 1912, particularly those who watched the lucky ones leave. She started to cry and could not stop. The only music heard throughout the film is that played by the ship's orchestra.

A NIGHT TO REMEMBER (1958)

Most people's favourite *Titanic* film, this was the British adaption of Walter Lord's 1955 book about the disaster and starred Kenneth More as Second Officer Charles Lightoller and included a young, and uncredited, Sean Connery as a steerage passenger. Producer William MacQuitty was at *Titanic*'s 1911 launch, as a six-year-old, and remembered being most impressed. Various survivors visited the film in progress including second-class passenger Lawrence Beesley and first-class passenger Edith Russell who brought with her the musical pig that she had taken into her lifeboat and played to soothe the anxieties of the children beside her. In fact, Edith's

A movie poster for the classic film *A Night to Remember*.

toy pig was used in the film. Charles Lightoller's son and widow met with the actor Kenneth More to advise him how to play the hero. *Titanic*'s second officer had died on 8 December 1952, twelve years after proving himself once more when he took his yacht, *Sundowner*, to Dunkirk, saving 130 British servicemen and using evasive manoeuvres – learned from his RAF (Royal Air Force) son – to dodge fire from enemy aircraft. Charles' story was the inspiration for Mr Dawson in Christopher Nolan's 2017 film *Dunkirk*.

One of the technical advisors on *A Night to Remember* was *Titanic*'s Fourth Officer Joseph Boxhall, while legend has it that Helen, Captain Smith's daughter, visited the film set and was overcome with emotion because the actor playing her father, Laurence

SHE WAS 'ORNERY', HE SAID, AND HE HAD NO IDEA WHY.

Naismith, was the image of him.

With so much input by the survivors, it must have made it an emotional experience for all involved. The film received its world premiere on Thursday, 3 July 1958 at the Odeon in London's Leicester Square. It was not a huge hit at the box office but did receive critical acclaim, from both sides of the Atlantic, along with the 'Samuel Goldwyn International Award' at the 1959 Golden Globes.

Director Roy Ward Baker said afterwards that the only person who gave him any trouble was Tucker McGuire, the actress who played Molly Brown. She was 'ornery', he said, and he had no idea why.

TITANIC (1997)

Canadian filmmaker James Cameron is, amongst other things, a director, producer, screenwriter and deep-sea explorer. Probably it was his fascination with shipwrecks – along with the famous

Nicholas Noxin documentary *Secrets of the Titanic* – that resulted in his epic film *Titanic* starring Kate Winslet and Leonardo di Caprio.

In an interview with ABC News he mentions picking up a copy of Walter Lord's book *A Night to Remember* and explains how his initial interest developed, over the next seventeen years, into a fierce obsession until the film's release in 1997.

In the name of research, Cameron visited the wreck thirty-three times over fifteen years in his determination to discover exactly how the ship broke up and what happened after it hit the seabed.

Eighty-seven year old Gloria Stuart was the oldest actor to be nominated for an Oscar for her portrayal of the aged Rose. She also had the honour of being the only person on the film set who was alive in 1912.

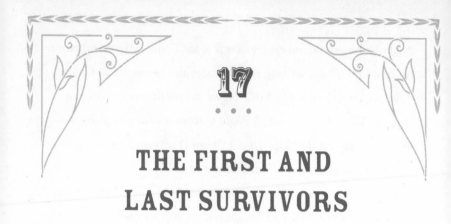

THE FIRST AND
LAST SURVIVORS

THE LAST TO LEAVE *TITANIC*

Amateur military historian, Colonel Archibald Gracie (1858–1912) may have been the very last survivor to leave the ship but he died eight months later due to, his family felt, his traumatic experience. He was one of the first up on deck after *Titanic* hit the iceberg and reported a Mr Stengel jokingly handing out bits of ice to keep as souvenirs. After a while, he and a friend noticed a list in the ship but decided against saying anything for fear of causing a commotion.

In between the order to evacuate and the final plunge of the ship, the colonel did all he could to help women, children and babies into the lifeboats. Offering his services to the first-class women around him, he guided them to the lifeboats and, of his small group, only Edith Evans was lost because she allowed her friend, Mrs Caroline Brown, to take her seat instead. The colonel had been prevented from accompanying the ladies up to the lifeboat, because men were not allowed near it, and he believed that

Edith must have fainted or was too afraid to make the climb into the boat and shouldered the guilt that he had not been there to encourage her.

Incredibly, Colonel Gracie was clinging to a railing as *Titanic* sank, he was pulled down with her but managed at last to let go. He found himself in a violent swirl of water and worried about being boiled alive when the boilers released their hot water. It was perhaps this worry alone that motivated him to start swimming for the surface. On breaking through, he found himself surrounded by debris and bodies and heard the cries of the dying.

He made a grab for wreckage and then spied an upturned collapsible boat in the distance and swam for it. One of the first to reach it, he was pulled aboard by the crew members that included Second Officer Lightoller.

On giving evidence at the American 1912 Senate Investigation, the colonel assured the judge that he would not want to hear gruesome details about the dying. Instead he told how the crew decided that they had to get their collapsible away from the panicked crowd who might topple them into the ocean. In short, they had no alternative, they felt, except to ignore people screaming for help and get away from them as fast as possible. The men on this boat spent hours standing in freezing water and escaped into other lifeboats as the sun rose on the morning of 15 April.

After his rescue by *Carpathia*, the colonel was unable to put the tragedy behind him and embarked on a book about the sinking, entitled *The Truth About Titanic*, which is still in print today. He tracked down as many survivors as he could and went to all the US hearings for the official record. He died just before the book went to the printers and during his last hours was heard to call out 'We must get them all into the boats.' The colonel was the first adult survivor to die. Many survivors attended his funeral including those he had saved.

THE LAST SURVIVING CREW MEMBER

Eighty-nine-year-old Sidney Daniels died on 25 May 1983, aged just over seventy-one, after he had survived as an eighteen-year-old steward on *Titanic*. He had worked on *Olympic,* impressing his superiors with his diligence, and was on board for her collision with HMS *Hawke*.

On 14 April 1912, a watchman woke him and told him to put on his life jacket and go up on deck. Ordered to help load the lifeboats, Sidney went to work until there was one boat left, Collapsible B, which was proving difficult to free from its ropes. Sidney climbed up near the bridge, saw the water lapping up the deck and, with no alternative, dived into the ocean to swim as fast as he could to avoid getting sucked down with the ship.

His mother had died the previous year, and he followed a star he could see in the night sky, believing it was her guiding him. Seeing a large shape in the distance, he swam towards it to discover it was the upturned Collapsible B. Climbing aboard, he found some space to sit down. He remembered praying with the other men until he told an older man next to him that he was tired and needed to sleep. Fortunately for him, the man ordered him to stay awake or else he would surely have died. On *Carpathia*, Sidney did not enjoy his first taste of coffee but kept drinking it to get warm.

He married his first wife in 1916, they had no children, and he was a widower two years later. He remarried in 1920, and this marriage lasted until his death on 25 May 1983, producing seven children, the remainder of which believe that they might be the last surviving offspring of a *Titanic* crewman.

THE LAST SURVIVOR

The death of ninety-seven-year-old Millvina Dean on 31 May 2009 was the end of an era for she was the last of the *Titanic* survivors.

Born on 2 February 1912, Elizabeth Gladys (Millvina) Dean was the youngest passenger on board and was travelling to America with her parents and brother, Bertram, because her father planned to open a tobacconist shop in Kansas. He died in the sinking and Millvina, her mother and brother sailed back on the *Adriatic* to England, where she unknowingly was a celebrity as nobody could believe that something so tiny had survived. People literally queued to hold her for a couple of moments, not that she knew this. In fact, she did not know she had been on *Titanic* until she was eight years old and her mother was getting married again. Millvina never married but achieved celebrity status once more, in her seventies, appearing in *Titanic* documentaries and as guest of honour at numerous exhibitions. In 1997, she was invited to finish her family's 1912 journey to Kansas, on the *QE2* and, then, in 1996, she visited Belfast for the first time, as special guest of a Titanic Historical Society convention. Bertram, her brother, had died on 14 April 1992 from pneumonia, on the eightieth anniversary of the collision with the iceberg.

She spent her last years in a nursing home in Southampton and was in the headlines again when it was discovered that she could no longer pay the fees. Don Mullan, the Irish journalist

PEOPLE LITERALLY QUEUED TO HOLD HER FOR A COUPLE OF MOMENTS, NOT THAT SHE KNEW THIS.

and photographer, included her portrait in his 2009 exhibition, *A Thousand Reasons for Living*. He also took a photograph of Millvina's hands as she signed her name and, to raise further funds for Millvina, he sold a limited edition of the picture at €500 a pop, challenging those behind the 1997 blockbuster *Titanic* movie to match his efforts financially. Consequently, the film's director, James Cameron, along with his two stars, Leonardo di Caprio and Kate Winslet, and singer Celine Dion, each donated $10,000 to the Millvina Dean Fund which had been set up by various *Titanic* societies to pay her nursing bills. She died shortly afterwards from pneumonia.

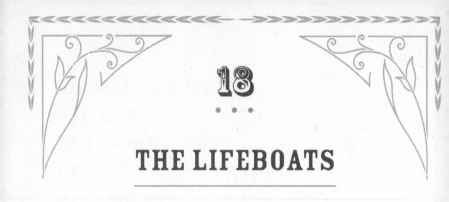

18

. . .

THE LIFEBOATS

There were twenty lifeboats on *Titanic* with spaces for 1,178 passengers and crew. In fact, this was more than the legal requirement which was sixteen lifeboats, space for 1,040 people. The following is a brief account of some of the stories attached to the boats. When facts about individual boats and their numbers of occupants vary, I stick to the findings on Encyclopedia Titanica (www.encyclopedia-titanica.org).

COLLAPSIBLE A (STARBOARD)

First-class passenger, Thomson Beattie, along with his two best friends, John Hugo Ross and Thomas McCaffry, left New York for Trieste, in January 1912, for a winter holiday. Goodness know what they got up to but, by March, Ross was ill and his exhausted companions were ready for home. Thomson wrote to tell his mother that they were sailing on the new unsinkable ship. He ended up in the unfortunate Collapsible A. This boat was not exactly launched as it entered the water at 2.15am, five minutes before *Titanic*'s final

THE "TITANIC'S" BOATS: WERE THEY TOO FAR FROM THE WATER?

DRAWN BY C. J. DE LACY.

↓ 75 FEET FROM BOAT DECK TO WATER.

"THE HEIGHT OF A GOOD-SIZED BLOCK OF FLATS": THE SPACE BETWEEN THE "TITANIC'S" BOAT-DECK AND THE SEA.

In the statement issued by a committee of surviving passengers of the "Titanic" appeared the following: "On the 'Titanic' the boat-deck was about 75 feet above water, and consequently the passengers were required to embark before the lowering of the boats, thus endangering the operation and preventing the taking on of the maximum number the boats would hold." Mr. Beasley's description, as well as those of others, makes it appear that passengers joined the boat also from B deck. On the same subject, Commander Crutchley, writing in the "Daily Telegraph," said: "It may be assumed that the 'Titanic's' boat-deck was, say, 70 feet from the water; in other words, the height of a good-sized block of flats . . . Imagine that a boat is being lowered from the top, and has reached, say, the level of the first floor, and realise, if you can, the feelings of the load of people that come in contact with that side when swinging, and then, if you care to, speculate (a) on the survival of the boat intact; (b) the likelihood of broken bones, or worse; and (c) the chance of the boat reaching the water undamaged."

plunge; instead, it floated off the ship, its canvas sides down, allowing the freezing water partially to submerge it and its desperate passengers. Thomson did not last the night, dying of exposure.

Meanwhile John Hugo Ross, ill with dysentery, on hearing that *Titanic* had struck an iceberg, returned to bed, convinced the situation was not serious, and declared it would take more than an iceberg to make him leave the ship. His body was never found.

Thomas McCaffry probably tried to follow Thomson into the collapsible but failed to do so. His body was later recovered by the *Mackay-Bennett*. Due, no doubt, to its calamitous launch, the facts are impossible to pin down. However, it is estimated that out of an initial thirty to forty people, only ten to twelve occupants survived the journey in Collapsible A, being transferred to Boat 14, while the dead were left behind. The little boat containing three decomposing corpses, including Thomson Beattie's, was found a month later, on 15 May, by RMS *Oceanic*, according to the *New York Tribune*, a hundred miles from the wreck site and when *Titanic* should have been making her second trip to New York. Thomson was buried at sea on his mother's birthday.

COLLAPSIBLE B (PORT)

At 11.50pm, on 14 April, Second Officer Charles Lightoller was summoned from his bed for the hardest and longest shift of his life. The next two hours flew by as he tirelessly filled lifeboats. Minutes before *Titanic's* final plunge, he resumed a battle to free Collapsible B from its ropes. Finally, he succeeded, but the little boat was instantly captured by the Atlantic. Out of options, Lightoller dived into the water and was dragged after *Titanic* into the darkness until a blast, caused by the icy water meeting the boilers, spat him back to the surface, right next to the now overturned Collapsible B. He climbed onto its back with possibly thirty others, again the numbers vary, including Colonel Gracie and telegrapher Harold Bride. Lightoller organised the men to forge a balance against the ocean swell. Within hours, the collapsible was almost sunk, the men by then up to their knees in water. Not surprisingly, at least three of them died, while the rest were – at *Carpathia*'s arrival – eventually divided between Lifeboats Nos. 4 and 12.

COLLAPSIBLE C (STARBOARD)

Launched at 2am, and the first collapsible to be lowered, 'C' is believed to have contained just under forty people, including six crew and Bruce Ismay. Before its release, either First Officer Murdoch or Chief Purser Hugh McElroy were obliged to fire a handgun twice in the air to deter men – some say they were a mix of stewards and third-class passengers – attempting to rush the boat. The shots brought first-class passengers Hugh Woolner and Björnstrom-Steffansön running and they physically dragged two men from the collapsible. *Titanic* had a severe list by now and the little boat had quite a rocky journey to the water.

COLLAPSIBLE D (PORT)

Collapsible D was the ninth boat to be launched from port side. Crew formed a barricade around this boat before its 2.05am release, only admitting women and children, thus obliging a father to bid farewell to his boys, three-year-old Michel and two-year-old Edmond. Mr Navratil had kidnapped his children from his estranged French wife but did not try to save himself. Post-disaster newspaper coverage of the 'Titanic orphans' helped their mother discover their whereabouts and she sailed to America to retrieve them. It could have held forty people but approximately twenty-five people were on board when it was lowered, although this number also ranges from nineteen to forty-four, depending on the survivor. Hugh Woolner and Björnstrom-Steffansön will leap into it from A deck and, in turn, they will rescue Frederick Maxfield Hoyt when he dives into the water alongside the boat. A photograph taken of this boat approaching *Carpathia* reveals a possible thirty occupants. Today, it is generally believed to have been half-full. One can only guess at the feelings of the bystanders who watched this collapsible leave, for there were only two boats left and over fifteen hundred passengers needing to be saved.

LIFEBOAT 1 (STARBOARD)

The fourth boat to be released from starboard, this was one of two small emergency cutters located either side of the ship, near the bridge. The cutters were already swung out, in preparation for instantly dealing with the likes of a crew member falling into the ocean. Capable of holding forty passengers, this boat's claim to fame is that it was released after 1pm with just twelve occupants, including Sir Cosmo and Lady Duff-Gordon, the only two passengers to be questioned during the investigative hearings as to why there were so few in it and why it did not attempt to rescue anyone after *Titanic* sank. The boat was the second to be met by *Carpathia* at 4.10am.

LIFEBOAT 2 (PORT)

The second of the two cutters left *Titanic* at 1.45am and was the first to be rescued by *Carpathia* at 4.10am. There were approximately seventeen people, mostly women, on board. According to passenger Elisabeth Walton Allen, as she and other ladies queued to get into the lifeboat they were overtaken by some eighteen or nineteen men, that she called stokers, who climbed in first, prompting an officer – possibly First Officer Lightoller – to order them out at gunpoint, accusing them of cowardice and adding that he would love to see them thrown overboard. One man who braved a jump into the boat and possible recriminations was steerage passenger, Austrian Anton Kink, who could not resist the cries of his wife and daughter and leapt after them in pursuit and, thus, the whole family survived the sinking, a rarity in third class.

LIFEBOAT 3 (STARBOARD)

The number of occupants fluctuate between thirty-two and fifty though it was probably less than forty. In any case, here was another half-empty lifeboat designed to hold twice the amount it did. Under Officer Murdoch's supervision, the boat was released at 12.55am, the fourth to leave *Titanic*. At the Senate Investigation, when Fifth Officer HG Lowe, who believed there had been at least forty occupants, was asked why the boat was not filled to capacity, he replied that there did not seem to be anyone else around. Publisher Henry Sleeper Harper accompanied his wife into the boat and was accompanied in turn by his prize-winning Pekingese, Sun Yat-sen, and a twenty-seven-year-old Egyptian dragoman (guide or interpreter), Hamad Hassab, he had brought from Cairo as a joke. One wonders if any embarrassment was felt when the family paper *Harper's Weekly* informed its readers that the usual rule was observed on *Titanic* – women and children first – a rule beheld of decent men but then in the very next issue published an exclusive interview with Henry who not only saved himself but also his dog.

LIFEBOAT 4 (PORT)

The first lifeboat to be released portside, it was one of the last lifeboats to finally leave at 1.50am. Initially the plan was to lower this boat to A deck to allow passengers to board there but this was made virtually impossible due to the locked windows on the deck's promenade. Thirteen-year-old John Ryerson had a lucky escape when Officer Lightoller refused to allow him to follow his mother, two sisters and maids into the boat. His father, Arthur, stepped forward to highlight his son's youth. Lightoller let the boy on but was heard to mutter 'No more boys'. Quartermaster Walter Perkis took charge and this may possibly explain why this boat, after *Titanic* sank, immediately rowed back to rescue six or seven crew from the water, the only boat to respond so quickly. It also went to the aid of the upside-down collapsible boat. Consequently, when it was met by *Carpathia* it was carrying between fifty-five and sixty passengers.

LIFEBOAT 5 (STARBOARD)

This boat left at 12.43am which meant there was no rush to board it, as most passengers did not appreciate that *Titanic* was really sinking, plus it had a relatively long drop to the ocean. Again, the actual number of occupants swing wildly from fifty to thirty-four to forty; however, it is believed that it was carrying either thirty-five or thirty-six passengers. Officer Murdoch put a reluctant Third Officer Herbert Pitman in charge. Pitman was already having an eventful night. He had snapped at a man wearing carpet slippers, who was telling him what to do, not recognising him as White Star's president. Bruce Ismay would also annoy Officer Lowe who was working to lower the boat. At Ismay's insistent and premature

'Lower away! Lower away!' Lowe told the president to get the hell out of the way.

After *Titanic* sank, Pitman wanted to return to the scene and pick up survivors, but he was shouted down by the other occupants. Mrs Ruth Dodge, whose husband, Washington Dodge, refused to take a seat in her boat, even though other husbands climbed in with their wives, also wanted to try to rescue people and was so disgusted by her fellow passengers that, at the first opportunity, she switched to another lifeboat.

Pitman was likely scarred by the experience and, during the Senate investigation, he became agitated when asked to describe the cries of the dying. At his passengers' refusal to return, he tucked in the oars and 'lay quiet'. With great reluctance, he admitted to hearing moans for about an hour until finally there was silence.

LIFEBOAT 6 (PORT)

This boat was launched at 1.10am with approximately twenty-four passengers, mostly women, in place of sixty-five. Officer Lightoller put Quartermaster Robert Hichens in charge and ordered lookout Frederick Fleet to get in and help with the rowing. However, as the boat was being lowered, either the women or Hichens insisted on another oarsman so Lightoller called for experienced sailors resulting in Canadian yachtsman Major Arthur Godfrey Peuchen stepping forward to offer his services. He was the only man, aside from crew, that the stickler Lightoller allowed into a lifeboat and had to prove himself with a precarious climb down the ropes into the boat that cost him his wallet. Seemingly, this was an unhappy boat thanks to Hichens. When *Titanic* sank, most of his passengers, including American Margaret Brown, urged a return to rescue survivors, but the quartermaster bluntly refused saying there was no point since there would only be 'stiffs in the water', adding, 'It is our lives now, not theirs'. Afterwards, a couple of passengers mentioned Hichens's laziness, rudeness and constant swearing. On being asked by Major Peuchen to help with the rowing, Hichens only cared to remind everyone who was in charge and remained at the rudder to navigate, which was, according to the major, quite unnecessary on such a calm, starry night. Hichens denied any wrongdoing at the Senate investigation, claiming never to have used the word 'stiff' in all his life and neither could he remember any proposals to rescue anyone.

LIFEBOAT 7 (STARBOARD)

This was the first boat to leave *Titanic*, launched at 12.40am, and men were having a luckier time with Officer Murdoch who allowed both genders into his lifeboats. Later, a first-class gentleman explained how an officer had asked him to get into the boat to encourage the reluctant women.

At the Senate investigations, Mrs Helen Bishop testified that there were twenty-eight people in this boat (there may have been twenty-nine) and that her husband had been pushed in with her. She was one of twelve women, the rest were men, three of whom were crew, and she was full of praise for their behaviour. She described the men in her boat as 'wonderful', mentioning how one man, whose brother remained on *Titanic*, put his head in his hands as the ship sank, but afterwards endeavoured to distract the ladies and keep them cheerful. Lookout George Hogg, who was in charge of the boat, returned Mrs Bishop's compliments when he told Senator Smith that he felt all the women deserved gold medals and promised he would, from now on, always raise his hat to a woman.

LIFEBOAT 8 (PORT)

This boat was launched at 1am, the first from portside, with twenty-seven or twenty-eight people in it. Such was the innocence at this stage that, as Mrs J Stuart White climbed into the boat, crewmen joked that she would need a pass to get back on *Titanic* the next morning. Furthermore, a light was spotted in the distance and the men were ordered to row towards it, deposit the passengers there and return to *Titanic* to pick up more. Mrs White was annoyed by some stewards who, on reaching the water, lit up cigarettes and pipes.

Able Seaman Thomas Jones commanded the boat and noticing the self-assurance of Lucy Noël Martha Leslie, otherwise known as the Countess of Rothes, asked her to steer and a friendship was born. Afterwards, the Countess presented Thomas with an inscribed silver watch, while he had the brass number '8' removed from their lifeboat, framed and sent to her. They wrote to one another at least once a year until her death in September 1956.

LIFEBOAT 9 (STARBOARD)

Launched at 1.30am, there are large discrepancies in reports of how many people were on board. The boat contained mostly second-class women, under the command of Boatswain Mate Albert Haines. Haines believed he had over fifty, although the crew, from boat to boat, tended to believe that they had more passengers than they did. It is thought that there were maybe forty or so occupants, including eighteen crew.

Twenty-four-year-old Léontine Aubart was travelling in first class with her maid and thousands of francs worth of dresses, hats and jewels because she believed no self-respecting Parisian woman could buy clothes in America. A nightclub singer, Mme Aubart was the mistress of married millionaire Benjamin Guggenheim who was travelling in a separate cabin. After seeing her and Emma, the maid, safely into Lifeboat 9, Guggenheim and his valet Victor Giglio, the story goes, returned to their cabins to put on their evening wear to die like gentlemen.

First-class steward Henry Samuel Etches, who tended to the likes of Thomas Andrews and the wealthy passengers, was ordered to take an oar in Lifeboat 5 and was asked by Guggenheim to tell his wife that he had done his duty. On reaching New York, Etches did exactly that, making his way to the St Regis Hotel to personally deliver the message to the newly widowed Florette. However, she was too upset to see him so he spoke to her brother-in-law, Daniel Guggenheim.

LIFEBOAT 10 (PORT)

Officer Murdoch launched this boat at 1.50am, putting it in the care of Able Seaman Edward Buley. *Titanic's* hard listing to port almost caused a separate tragedy when a woman fell through the sudden gap that opened up between the ship and the lifeboat. Miraculously, she was pulled to safety on the deck below.

Chief Baker Charles Joughin was assigned to this boat but, at the last moment, decided differently. Having been woken by the impact of the collision, he left his cabin to see what was wrong. Based on vague information, he assembled his thirteen bakers and had them deliver four loaves of bread to every lifeboat. Then he returned to his cabin for a nip of whiskey and, by 12.30am, was back at Lifeboat 10, helping women and children into it. On noticing some women running off, out of fear, he gave chase, manhandling them back and into the boat. Deciding there were enough men to take care of the rowing, he did not leave *Titanic*, feeling that to have done so would have set a bad example. Instead, he had another drink. He ended up in the ocean, as *Titanic* sank, but was a strong swimmer and was also fortified by the whiskey in his gut which may have helped him survive the freezing temperatures for two hours until he was pulled up onto the overturned Collapsible B.

LIFEBOAT 11 (STARBOARD)

Another of Officer Murdoch's lifeboats, this was lowered at 1.35am with Able Seaman Sidney Humphreys in command. It held somewhere between fifty and seventy passengers with one woman so crazed in her efforts to get into it that she fell in on top of the man trying to help her.

Masseuse Maude Slocombe had had plenty to do after she arrived on *Titanic* to find half-eaten sandwiches and empty beer bottles in the Turkish Bath, her work station, left there by the Harland & Wolff workers. Sitting in Lifeboat 11, she watched *Titanic*'s last plunge, noting the gradual loss of the lights and heard the band play 'Nearer My God to Thee.'

Another passenger was eleven-month-old Hudson Trevor Allison, the only survivor of his first-class family, with his nurse Alice Cleaver. They had become separated from his parents and two-year-old sister Lorraine, who was the only child to die from first and second class.

LIFEBOAT 12 (PORT)

This boat was released at 1.30am under the charge of Able Seamen Frederick Clench and John Poingdestre with approximately thirty passengers, mostly woman and children. It was rowed about a quarter of a mile from the sinking ship, from where Clench watched *Titanic* sink, bow first, all her lights out. When the screaming and shouting started, he convinced the frightened women beside him that it was just the occupants of the other lifeboats keeping in touch with one another. After *Titanic* disappeared, Lifeboat 12 was strung together with boats 10, 4 and Collapsible D, under the command of Fifth Officer Harold Godfrey Lowe who emptied out his passengers amongst the others and returned to rescue as many as he could. When he left, Clench's attention was caught by the peculiar sight of men standing on what he thought was a ship's funnel. This was Officer Lightoller's exhausted group who had been performing a balancing act for the past hour or so on the back of Collapsible B. Both Lifeboats 12 and 4 made their way to them and those tired men were finally able to sit down.

LIFEBOAT 13 (STARBOARD)

This boat was launched at 1.40am with sixty-five occupants who, on reaching the water, were obliged to shout out as they saw Lifeboat 15 being lowered directly on top of them. First-class dining-room steward Frederick D Ray was fond of the Dodge family and determined to save Washington Dodge's life. He spied the doctor nearby and, on hearing that Mrs Dodge and their five-year-old son had left on another lifeboat, Ray shoved the doctor into Lifeboat 13, his boat. He had served them on the *Olympic* and felt responsible for their predicament since he had encouraged them to travel home to America on the new *Titanic*. He came to their aid once more on the *Carpathia*. Mrs Dodge had no idea her husband had survived and never saw him in the crowd of survivors, but her son did and behaved as five-year-olds do, thinking it was a game to hide from his father, and did not share his discovery with his mother. Ray brought about the family reunion which must have been a joy to watch.

LIFEBOAT 14 (PORT)

Launched at 1.25am with approximately fifty-eight people, mostly women and children, on board, this boat was under the command of Fifth Officer Harold Godfrey Lowe. With panic growing, Lowe found it necessary to fire his revolver three times to stop any men thinking about jumping into the boat. In the Atlantic, he rounded up four other boats and distributed his passengers amongst them, leaving his boat empty for rescuing those in the water. However, Lowe felt it necessary to wait awhile. He was grilled on this point by Senator Smith, during the American investigation, and explained his decision that it would have been suicide to row his boat into a mass of people who would swamp him and, so, he allowed about an hour to pass before returning to the site of the sinking. He pulled four people out of the water including an overweight Mr William Fisher Hoyt who was in a bad way, bleeding from his nose and mouth, and sadly died just before *Carpathia* arrived.

LIFEBOAT 15 (PORT)

This boat was launched at 1.41am, lowered simultaneously with

Lifeboat 13, with Fireman Frank Dymond in charge. With sixty-five passengers, this was one of the fullest boats, and Officer Murdoch had to repeatedly remind the anxious crowd that it was women and children first.

Swede Mrs Selma Augusta Emilia Asplund was in this lifeboat along with Felix, her three-year-old son, and Lilian, her five-year-old daughter. However, it must have been agonising to leave behind Carl, her husband, and their other children: thirteen-year-old Filip, nine-year-old Clarence and five-year-old Carl (Lilian's twin). Why Carl or Clarence were not with her is just one of many questions that remain unanswered today. Neither Lillian nor Felix ever married, they stayed together with their mother and never ever spoke about the tragedy. Fifty-two years later, Mrs Asplund died on 15 April 1964 and, then, with the death of ninety-nine-year old Lillian, in 2006, who had outlived her brother by twenty-three years, the last survivor with actual memories of *Titanic* was gone. David Brown from the *Washington Post* spent some time with Lilian before her death, but she spoke very little about the ship, only mentioning how the smell of the fresh paint bothered her and that the people on *Carpathia* were very kind to her. She had spent her life declining invitations to talk about *Titanic*, explaining that her mother did not want her to remember anything. As Brown surmises, there is much to be said in silence; the Asplund family in their own way remind us how dreadfully sad the tragedy was.

LIFEBOAT 16 (STARBOARD)

Launched at 1.20am, with approximately fifty occupants, mostly women and children from second and third class, this boat was under the command of Master-at-Arms Henry Joseph Bailey who had to shimmy down the ropes to reach it. One of two Master-at-Arms, Bailey and his colleague Thomas Walter King, who did not survive, were responsible for law and order, and it is peculiar that Bailey was never asked to testify at either of the inquiries.

One of his passengers was Violet Jessop, the twenty-four-year-old stewardess who had barely cheated death when she survived a childhood bout of tuberculosis. She was on *Olympic* for her 1911 collision with HMS *Hawke*, and one might imagine that surviving the *Titanic* sinking the following year was enough drama for any lifetime yet, four years later, Jessop inadvertently took part in *Britannic*'s final journey. This time her lifeboat did not provide certain rescue due to the ship's raised propellers. She narrowly avoided being sliced up by jumping into the sea, receiving a blow to the head when she was sucked beneath the ship's keel. Years later, she visited a doctor about her bad headaches and was told that she must have, at some stage, fractured her skull. She died in 1971, at the age of eighty-three.

RMS *Carpathia* had only room for 13 lifeboats and, on reaching New York, these boats were lined up in the White Star Line spot, where *Titanic* should have been docked. Presumably they were recycled once they were stripped of their *Titanic* signage. Following the investigative hearings, ships now had to carry enough lifeboats for all souls on board, and it is possible that these 13 boats – which had carried hundreds of people to the safety of *Carpathia* – ended up joining their counterparts on *Olympic*.

Titanic's lifeboats docked in New York harbour, in place of *Titanic*.

19

• • •

THE RESCUE SHIPS OF THE LIVING AND THE DEAD

RMS *CARPATHIA*: CAPTAIN ARTHUR ROSTRON AND HIS SHIP OF SORROW

Rather chilling is the fact that, but for Harold Cottam awaiting news from another ship and, therefore, keeping his headphones on after he had finished his shift, there would have been no such thing as a *Titanic* survivor.

On the night of 14 April 1912, Captain Arthur Rostron was woken up by Cottam, his wireless operator, to be told that *Titanic* was in distress. He immediately had his ship set course for the liner's position, approximately fifty-eight miles away, at a maximum speed of seventeen knots per hour, three knots faster than her normal speed. Four days into her voyage, *Carpathia* was on her way from New York to Trieste and her 1,000 passengers slept on as her crew readied the ship to receive what they imagined would be 2,000 more. Blankets were fetched, tables were laid for umpteen cups of hot soup, tea and coffee, while sleeping areas were designated, including the library, saloons and smoking rooms.

Margaret Brown presents Captain Rostron with his loving cup on behalf of the grateful survivors.

First Aid Stations were set up in the three dining rooms, each with its own doctor and *Carpathia*'s crew were advised to have some hot coffee themselves for the long night ahead. A seaman for twenty-seven years, Captain Rostron had been with Cunard for seventeen of those years and this was his second year as a Cunard captain and only his third month on *Carpathia*. Once his orders were given, he prayed; his Christian faith was of huge importance to him. His second officer, James Bisset, in the second volume of his memoir, *Tramps and Ladies – My Early Years in Steamers* (1959), related a conversation he had with his pious captain when Rostron described as blasphemous the newspapers' bragging about *Titanic* being unsinkable.

At the 1912 Senate investigation, Harold Cottam related the last message he ever received from *Titanic*, 'Come quick, our engine room is filling up to the boilers.'

To push his ship as fast as she would go, Captain Rostron had the hot water and heating turned off, making more steam for the engines. According to James Bisset, the last eight miles were nerve-wracking and he praised Captain Rostron for his daring, to push *Carpathia* at full speed, relying on his lookouts to spy icebergs in enough time to avoid them, while everyone longed for daylight as the hours ticked by. *Carpathia* finally arrived after 4am, on 15 April, almost two hours after *Titanic* sank, to spend the next four hours or so rescuing those in the lifeboats, taking 13 of the boats on board. Lifeboat 2 was the first to reach *Carpathia* and Elisabeth Walton Allen the first to brave the climb to the deck, while the first crewman, Joseph Boxhall, *Titanic*'s Fourth Officer, was rushed to Captain Rostron who demanded to know where *Titanic* was. It is not easy to imagine the shock at Boxhall's reply, 'She's gone, sank at 2.20am.'

James Bisset describes the state of the survivors; some of them were dreadfully seasick and most were numb from the cold, too lightly dressed for the freezing temperatures. Some of them wept and many lacked the energy to climb the ladders to the rescuer's deck; children, for instance, had to be placed inside canvas bags and hauled up the side of *Carpathia*.

While searching for more lifeboats, *Carpathia*'s crew and passengers peered over the ship's railings, transfixed by the scene around them, the only evidence of a dead body in the brief flash of white of a life jacket, since the rest of the person was just about submerged.

One man described how a Portuguese bride mistook the rescue ship for *Titanic* and had to be physically restrained from flinging herself overboard when her husband's loss could not be denied. She was just one of the many brides and wives who found themselves widowed by the practically unsinkable liner.

Another story that appeared in the *Daily Sketch* newspaper, on 6 May, concerned an army officer who saw his mother fall out of one of the collapsible boats. He dived into the freezing water and spent over an hour searching for her body amongst the corpses. Finally, just as he was succumbing himself to the Atlantic, he was hauled into a lifeboat.

As *Titanic's* lifeboats were found and emptied, the survivors from earlier boats, would check to see if their husband, father, brother was amongst the new arrivals. What else was there to do but hope that your loved one had been saved until you knew for sure otherwise? Consequently, the rescue of the last lifeboat from *Titanic*, was like the sounding of the death knell for all those who realised that their loved ones were not amongst the final group.

Captain Rostron had a difficult decision to make as to whether he should collect the dead from the ocean before deciding that the survivors had been through enough, without the distressing sight of bodies that would need to be identified, and *Carpathia* set off for New York. With approximately 705 extra passengers on board. The atmosphere was sombre and all the usual entertainment was cancelled, while survivors would spend hours staring at the ocean in disbelief and shock. Inside the Marconi Office, however, the situation was anything but mute.

Obviously, Captain Rostron's priority was to have the survivors named as quickly as possible and for that list to be relayed to the New York White Star office. He was conscious about anxious relatives that could do nothing but wait. And so, telegrapher Harold Cottam set about transmitting the list of names, with what must have been an agonising attention to detail, but found himself hampered by the 150-mile range of *Carpathia's* radio set which meant his messages were not getting through. Meanwhile, he was besieged by hundreds of telegrams wanting to know if such-and-such had survived and was also obliged to field dozens of different newspapers demanding details on *Titanic*'s demise. Furthermore, there were the survivors themselves needing him to message their families to say they were safe. Cottam worked solidly, without a break, for the next couple of days until Harold Bride, *Titanic*'s junior wireless officer, still suffering from shock and exposure, arrived to help, thus allowing Cottam to grab a few hours of sleep.

Newspaper editors were bewildered when Captain Rostron forbade any communication with the press. Hysterical accusations of censorship were made against the captain who would have guessed that there would be an official investigation into the sinking. Still, wily reporters promised huge sums of cash to the telegraphers in exchange for an exclusive interview.

Allegedly, on arriving in New York, Harold Bride gave an interview to *The New York Times*, for which he may have been paid between $500 to $1000, which was worth at least a couple of years of his salary. The interview may have been arranged by his boss, Guglielmo Marconi, who had contacts with *The New York Times*.

James Bisset gives a wonderful account of *Carpathia*'s entrance to New York Harbour at about 6pm, Thursday, 18 April. The ship was met by a sizeable fleet of assorted boats bulging with delirious newspapermen, concerned relatives and curious onlookers. Captain Rostron sensibly delegated his crew to personally block every entrance to ensure that no one boarded his ship, aside from the pilot who would guide *Carpathia* into the harbour. When the journalists realised this there was outrage. At least one officer was obliged to sock a few aggressive reporters in the jaw. With bruised faces, they continued to plead, offering money and then pretending their family was on board. As they neared the port, *Carpathia's* crew suddenly realised the immensity of the situation when they discerned a crowd of maybe 30,000 waiting for them in the rain.

At some point, Captain Rostron was ambushed by one unpleasant reporter who somehow managed to sneak on board. Completely oblivious to the grief and the great loss suffered, he repeatedly and gleefully exclaimed, 'What a story! Oh boy, what a story!' before following up with such ridiculous questions as to whether it was true that *Titanic's* crew had shot dead the third-class women and children so that the millionaires could board the lifeboats.

Almost immediately, stories were written about the disaster. However, some were pure fiction like the one that appeared in the *Montreal Herald* on 19 April that had sculptor Paul Chevre describe seeing both Captain Smith blow his brains out with his revolver and Archibald Butt, President Taft's personal aide, shoot dead seven men who were trying to get into a lifeboat. Three days later, an enraged Chevre arrived at the *Herald's* office to denounce the story as a fake.

Carpathia returned to work almost as soon as Captain Rostron finished testifying at the Senate investigation, for which he received a round of applause. Bissett says that at every stop, the captain was feted as a hero. When they returned to New York, seven weeks later, Bissett was given the task of sifting through Captain Roston's enormous pile of fan mail that included more than one marriage proposal. The captain was also summoned to the White House to receive the highest honour in the land, that of the Congressional Medal of Honour from President Taft. The rest of the crew received their share of glory, from a bonus of two months' extra pay to gold or silver medals, depending on rank, that were engraved with *Carpathia* surrounded by icebergs, being approached by five *Titanic* lifeboats under the watchful eye of King Neptune. The captain received many more honours including a Loving Cup (a two-handled trophy) from the committee of *Titanic*'s survivors, as headed by Mrs Margaret Brown, and a gold medal and certificate from the Liverpool Shipwreck and Humane Society.

Unfortunately, the ship herself did not have a happy ending. She sank after being hit by two torpedoes on 17 July 1918, on her way to Boston. A third torpedo hit while the lifeboats were being put out, killing five crew. By that stage, Captain Rostron had been transferred to other ships. When he retired in 1931, he wrote his own memoir, *Home from the Sea*. Captain Arthur Rostron died from pneumonia on 4 November 1940.

THE *MACKAY-BENNET*: THE FUNERAL SHIP

The *Mackay-Bennet*, a cable-laying ship, had the dubious honour of being commissioned by White Star Line to search for the bodies for a daily rate of US $550. She left Halifax on 18 April with approximately 600 pinewood coffins, an undertaker, a clergyman and enough embalming fluid for 70, which was all that was available. Newspapers reported that she found 100 bodies on 24 April of which 27 were identified. Meanwhile, mail ships were advised to steer clear of the area as it became clear that bodies had drifted far from the site.

James Bisset, second officer on *Carpathia*, wrote about how the area was believed to be haunted and, so, was avoided by other vessels. Medical opinion, that is, the doctor on *Mackay-Bennett*, upheld that the deaths had been instantaneous and, furthermore, most of the bodies would never surface again. However, this theory of instant death contradicts the likes of Third Officer Pitman who claimed he heard shouts and cries for a whole hour after *Titanic* sank.

Apparently, there were more bodies than expected and Captain Lardner's request for a second ship was answered in the form of the cable steamer *Minia*. Two other ships were also involved in the search, the *Montmagny* and the *Algerine*. The *Mackay-Bennet* conducted a search across thirty miles of the site, the captain remarking on how most of the bodies were found upright in the water as if they were swimmers resting awhile. The site was strewn with doors, cushions, chairs and bits of wreckage. Several men were in evening dress and, for the most part, the bodies were bunched together as if seeking companionship in the freezing waters. One group was comprised of 100 bodies. Frederick Hamilton, an engineer on board the ship, wrote how 51 bodies were recovered on 21 April: 46 men, 3 women and 2 children. One of the children, a toddler, could not be identified and was christened 'Our Babe' by the crew. In all, a total of 306 bodies were recovered, far too many for the limited supply of embalming fluid on board and, in any case, the *Daily Sketch* wrote how 116 bodies were badly mutilated thereby making it impossible to identify them. Faces were bruised and cut whilst limbs were fractured or broken. There was talk of a possible explosion causing the injuries. Eighteen women were found but none were judged to be from first class. Furthermore, none of the bodies bore proof of having been shot.

On 20 April, Steamship *Bremen* was on her way from Bremen to New York, a route that took her right through the area where *Titanic* went down. First-class passenger Mrs Johanna Stunke wrote about what happened next. Initially, *Bremen*'s passengers were impressed by the sight of a huge iceberg glistening in the afternoon sunshine but then there was considerable distress over the sighting of approximately 200 bodies in the water, including that of a mother whose arms still held her baby. The captain told the *Chicago Daily Tribune* that he counted 125 before feeling too upset to carry on. Mrs Stunke also mentions seeing a woman with her arms around a dog, possibly a Saint Bernard. Several people demanded that the *Bremen* stop to collect the bodies but they were assured that the *Mackay-Bennet* was on her way to look after them.

Lacking the facilities for so many bodies, Canon Kenneth Cameron Hind from All Saints' Cathedral, conducted over 100 sea burials on the *Mackay-Bennett* in three separate services. Afterwards Hind praised the crew for coping so well under the physical and emotional strain.

THERE WAS CONSIDERABLE DISTRESS OVER THE SIGHTING OF APPROXIMATELY 200 BODIES IN THE WATER, INCLUDING THAT OF A MOTHER WHOSE ARMS STILL HELD HER BABY.

Bad weather brought the search to an end, and the *Mackay-Bennett* returned to Halifax on the morning of 30 April, unloading her cargo at about 9.30am. She had found the most bodies, the *Minia* had found 17 while the *Montmagny* and the *Algerine* would go on to find 4 and 1 respectively. In June, the clergyman aboard the *Montmagny*, the last ship to find bodies, believed that the cork life jackets were disintegrating, thus releasing the bodies to the ocean floor.

'Our Babe', the unidentified child, one of the first bodies to be recovered by the *Mackay-Bennett*, was interred in Halifax's Fairview Lawn Cemetery. Estimated to be about two years of age, he was wearing a grey coat, brown frock, petticoat, pink vest, brown shoes and stockings. No one came forward to claim him and, therefore, the crew took care of him; they not only escorted the little coffin to its final resting place, they paid for the erection of a large memorial to 'An Unknown Child'. The funeral was the only one to take place on 4 May 1912. One crew member, twenty-four-year-old Clifford Crease, laid a wreath on the grave every 15 April for years afterwards.

A brass plate was put in with the body which helped to identify the child in later years in that it accidentally sheltered a piece of bone. In 2002, he was mistakenly identified as Finnish toddler Eino Viljam(i) Panula by an American television programme using the bone fragment. Six years later, thanks to improvements in DNA analysis, he was eventually and correctly named as third-class passenger Sidney Leslie Goodwin. The reason that nobody claimed him back in 1912 was because his entire family, two parents, two sisters and three brothers, had been lost in the sinking.

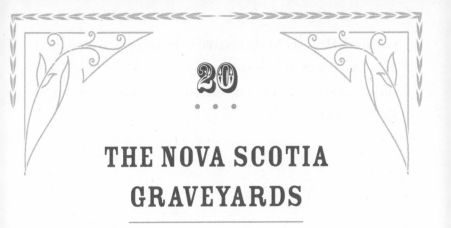

THE NOVA SCOTIA
GRAVEYARDS

It was White Star Line who paid for the headstones that went up during the autumn of 1912. The *Titanic* bodies, those not claimed by relatives, were divided between three different graveyards, the biggest share going to the Fairview Lawn Cemetery. Here, 121 bodies are buried with 42 remaining unidentified. A gentle sloping of the ground made it necessary to lay the headstones out in three curved lines, reminiscent of the curve of a ship's bow.

One of the *Titanic* occupants is Jack Dawson whose grave, thanks to Leonardo di Caprio's fictional namesake in the 1997 film *Titanic*, perhaps rivals Jim Morrison's grave in Père Lachaise with hundreds of visitors leaving flowers and trinkets around it.

The second graveyard, the Mount Olivet Catholic Cemetery's *Titanic* plot contains 19 victims, including Mrs Margaret Rice from Athlone, Ireland, who was travelling with her five young sons, none of whom were ever found. Four victims were never identified.

The third graveyard is the Baron de Hirsch Jewish Cemetery which holds ten *Titanic* victims. Out of the ten, only two were ever identified. Here lies Michel Navratil, the father who absconded from France with his two young sons but at least got his children safely into a lifeboat. He had boarded *Titanic* under the name of Louis M Hoffman.

21
. . .

TITANIC BELFAST

THE SS *NOMADIC*

Designed by Thomas Andrews, the SS *Nomadic*, a White Star Line tender, came into being on Slipway no. 1, in 159 days, in the shadow of her neighbour, the immense Arrol Gantry housing the potentials that would be *Olympic* and her younger sister. The *Nomadic* was launched on 25 April 1911 to carry passengers, their baggage and mail to and from *Olympic* and *Titanic*. Over a century and more than one renovation later, she's an integral part of the Titanic Experience in Belfast today. Indeed, it is quite something to step aboard one of the two ships, the other being SS *Traffic*, that ferried *Titanic*'s first and second–class passengers out to her from Cherbourg harbour.

Approximately 274 passengers stepped onto the *Nomadic* on 10 April 1912, perhaps impatient to exchange the little ship for the biggest and grandest ship the world had ever seen. However, the *Nomadic* was no 'plain Jane', and carried plenty of decorative extras like cushioned benches and porcelain water fountains, for the likes of the Astors, the Duff-Gordons and Benjamin Guggenheim.

White Star Line tender SS *Nomadic* is now part of Belfast Titanic Experience.

During the war, she ferried a different class of people – American soldiers – under her new employer, the French government, who also sent her out on minesweeping and patrol duties. After 1918, she was a tender once more and, in 1927, was sold to Compagnie Cherbourgeoise de Transbordement. Seven years later, she was sold to the Cherbourg Tow and Rescue Service and renamed *Ingenieur Minard*.

The Second World War saw her helping to evacuate Cherbourg before moving to Portsmouth Harbour for a new employer, the Royal Navy, where she resumed previous military duties: transporting soldiers, patrolling waters and minesweeping. But she would see Cherbourg again after war damage ensured that ships could not dock at the harbour and a tender was required once more. She was retired in 1968 and lay around for five long years before embarking on a rather glamourous role, for new owner Yvon Vincent, as a floating restaurant, a party vessel, in the Seine, Paris.

She needed rescuing after Vincent's death in 2005, to divert her from the scrapyard; and rescued she was, thanks to a marvellous effort by enthusiasts such as the Belfast Titanic Society, the French Titanic Society and the Save Nomadic Appeal, whose hard work paid off when in 2006 Northern Ireland's Department for Social Development stepped in to buy the *Nomadic* for £25,001. She returned to Belfast, her birthplace, in dire need of a complete revamp, and the Nomadic Charitable Trust, her new owner, was created to oversee the job. Once transformed she was handed over to her current owner, the Titanic Foundation, in April 2015. She is a genuine piece of *Titanic* and White Star Line history.

TITANIC BELFAST

Belfast Lough watched the building of *Titanic* and today the lough plays witness to her legacy. Since it opened in March 2012, Titanic Belfast has welcomed over three million visitors from all over the world. In December 2016, Titanic Belfast won a million votes worldwide, beating the Eiffel Tower, Giant's Causeway and *everything* else to become the World's Leading Tourist Attraction. Unfortunately, the designer, Texan Eric Kuhne, had suffered a fatal heart attack a few months previously, but he left behind the most wonderful narrative of a century's worth of Belfast's ship-building history.

Titanic Belfast.

On approaching Titanic Belfast, one is immediately captivated by its shape and texture. From above, the building is star-shaped, with four prongs that, seen from the ground, makes one think of a ship's bow and hull. The four sides of the museum shimmer in the sun, to remind us of frozen water crystallising and forming deadly but beautiful icebergs. So, yes, we note the ship's bows, all four of them, but also, we are to think of the immense Arrol Gantry, the superstructure that housed the births of *Olympic* and *Titanic*. In fact, those four sides represent the four ages of shipbuilding in Belfast – Wood, Iron, Steel and Aluminium. You can see the slipways out back; visit at night and the outlines of the two ships are lit up in blue, your imagination fills in the rest.

Keep in mind that eight lives were lost here, during *Titanic*'s construction, the very first being fifteen-year-old catch-boy Samuel Joseph Scott who fell twenty-three feet from the side of *Titanic* to his death on 20 April 1910. Water surrounds the museum, like a medieval moat, reflecting the futuristic triangles, each one unique, that form the outer husk of the building, along with nature's finest, the Belfast sky.

Follow *Titanic*'s route in the pavement outside. Rest yourself on a bench, not one of them is randomly placed, instead they form the dots and dashes of *Titanic*'s distress call, SOS CQD, in Morse code. Out front there is the giant '*Titanic*' sign, reminiscent of Los Angeles' 'Hollywood', cut from the same 2.5 cm steel plate that was used to build the ship. Goodness knows how many photographs it has appeared in.

Inside, the entire story of *Titanic*, *Olympic* and Belfast is encapsulated across six floors that are stacked like the decks of a ship. Be warned, time will fly. On a busy day, the noise can be tremendous and it is easy to be distracted by the cafes, the shop and sheer crowds milling around the atrium, queuing for tickets, collecting tickets or waiting for their premium tour to commence. A variety of languages and accents reminds you of the different nationalities that crop up in the list of passengers and will also impress upon you how many different people are still gripped by this ship of dreams. And, yet, this is just a building, a massive museum made over to the ghosts of a maiden voyage that lasted barely five days but it works. You can join the queues to gaze at the Mona Lisa, the Colosseum, the Vatican and the battlefields of the two world wars while the reason for this museum is two and a half miles down at the bottom of the Atlantic. And yet she is here, in spirit, along with her crew and passengers, as, deck by deck, you make your way deeper into the story.

Titanic and *Olympic* represented the pinnacle of shipbuilding's finest hour and perhaps one can say the same about *Titanic* Belfast.

TITANIC
EXPERIENCE COBH

Recipient of the 2015 Trip Advisor Certificate of Excellence, this little museum can be found in Casement Square, just past the promenade.

The building dates back to the early nineteenth century and was the original White Star Line ticket office where *Titanic*'s final passengers queued up on 11 April 1912. Of the 123 passengers waiting to be ferried out to *Titanic* at Roche's Point, 79 would lose their lives in the sinking.

The museum focuses on the Queenstown passengers and the tour includes the original White Star Line pier, also known as Heartbreak Pier, which was immortalised in Father Browne's famous photograph (see page 142).

A few minutes' walk away from the museum is the memorial garden in Cove Fort. Opened in 2013, the garden looks out onto Roche's Point and includes a wall of glass bearing the 123 names.

There is also a memorial stone, given to Cobh by Mrs Florence Ismay, wife of White Star Line director Bruce Ismay, which came from their garden in Costello Lodge, Connemara, County Galway.

Furthermore, there is a great tribute to *Titanic* in Cobh Heritage Centre, located within Cobh's restored Victorian railway station. It is well worth a visit. Aside from *Titanic,* the centre also explores the stories behind the thousands of Irish who left behind their homeland as a matter of necessity during the Irish Famine, or otherwise. Between 1845 and 1851, over a million people emigrated from Ireland, including young Annie Moore who was the first emigrant to be processed in Ellis Island, New York.

There is also the *Lusitania* exhibition, a reminder that Cobh has links to more than one shipping disaster. When a German submarine torpedoed the Cunard liner, RMS *Lusitania,* twenty kilometres off the coast of the Old Head of Kinsale, on 7 May 1917, there was not enough time to launch most of the lifeboats. In fact, only six boats were launched as it took just eighteen minutes for the ship to sink with the loss of over eleven hundred lives. Hundreds of bodies were taken out of the water, while others would be washed up on Cork's shores over the following weeks. Cobh's local boat owners made a valiant effort to save as many people as they could, but the tragedy all happened so fast. Today, you can visit the Old Church Cemetery, on the outskirts of Cobh, where the remains of 193 *Lusitania* victims were laid to rest.

BIBLIOGRAPHY/ SOURCES

PUBLICATIONS

Barratt, Nick: *Lost Voices from the Titanic*, St Martin's Press, New York, 2010

Berg, A Scott: *Max Perkins*, Simon & Schuster, UK, 2013

Bigham, Randy Bryan: *Finding Dorothy*, Lulu Press, US, 2012

Bryceson, Dave: *The Titanic Disaster*, PSL, UK, 1997

Chaplain, Charles: *My Autobiography*, Bodley Head, UK, 1964

Everett (ed), Marshall: *Story of the Wreck of the Titanic*, Dover Publications, NY, 2011

Gracie, Colonel Archibald: *Titanic, A Survivor's Story*, Sutton Publishing, UK, 1998

Green, Rod: *Building the Titanic*, Carlton Books, GB, 2005

Hall, Steve and Beard, Katie: *Titanic 101*, History Press, UK, 2013

Heyer, Paul: *Titanic Century: Media, Myth and the Making of a Cultural Icon*, Praeger, UK, 2012

Hill, Judith: *Lady Gregory: An Irish Life*, Sutton Publishing, UK, 2005

Hines, Stephen W: *Titanic: One Newspaper, Seven Days and the Truth That Shocked the World*, Cumberland House, US, 2011

Kuntz, Tom (ed): *The Titanic Disaster Hearings*, Pocket Books, NY, 1998

Lord, Walter: *A Night to Remember*, Penguin, England, 1978

Lord, Walter: *The Night Lives On*, Avon, US, 1998

McCaughan, Michael: *The Birth of the Titanic*, The Blackstaff Press, Belfast, 1998

O'Donnell, EE: *Father Browne's Titanic Album*, Wolfhound Press, Dublin, 1997

Pollard (ed), Arthur: *The Victorians*, Penguin, England, 1993

Robinson, W Sydney: *Muckraker, The Scandalous Life and Times of W.T. Stead*, The Robinson Press, Great Britain, 2013

Stead, WT: *The Blue Island*, Martino Publishing, UK, 2014

Tibballs, Geoff: *Voices from the Titanic*, Constable & Robinson, UK, 2012

White, John DT: *The RMS Titanic Miscellany*, Irish Academic Press, Dublin, 2012

Wilson, AN: *The Victorians*, Arrow Books, London, 2003

SOURCES

www.attackingthedevil.co.uk

www.beamly.com

www.biblio.com

www.biography.com

www.blogboxinghistory.org.uk

www.dogingtonpost.com

www.catholicherald.co.uk

www.chroniclingamerica.loc.gov

www.encyclopedia-titanic.org

www.fatherbrowne.com

www.fatherbyles.com

www.foxnews.com

www.hmhsbritannic.weebly.com

www.maritimemuseum.novascotia.ca

www.iran-times.com

www.nationalgraphic.com

www.ncregister.com

www.newworldencyclopedia.org

www.smithstownhistorical.org

www.ssmaritime.com

www.straushistoricalsociety.org

www.titanicfacts.net

www.titanic-passengers.com

www.titanicuniverse.com

www.venetianvase.co.uk

www.worldsquash.org

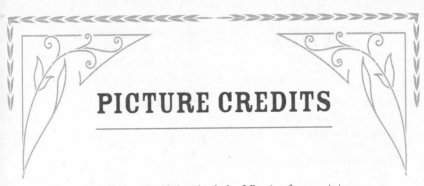

PICTURE CREDITS

The author and publisher thank the following for permission
to use photographs and illustrative material: front cover image: courtesy of
Mary Evans Picture Library; p121 Joan Barry (Fr Byles's great niece) & Christie
Seyglinski (for putting me in touch with her); p68, 173 Randy Bryan Bigham;
p78 Bournemouth News and Picture Service (BNPS); pp119, 144 Father
Browne Collection, Davison & Associates; p29 Steve Hall; p34 hmhsbritannic
website & Michail Michailakis; pp10, 19, 28, 39, 44, 60, 110, 204, 206 Library
of Congress; pp12, 20, 129, 159 Mary Evans Picture Library; pp73, 92, 101, 102,
165, 187 Mary Evans Picture Library and London Illustrated News; pp9, 44
Mary Evans Picture Library/Onslow Auctions Ltd; pp177, 220-1, 223
Shutterstock; p97 Joan Adler, Straus Historical Society; p181 Bill Wormstedt.
If any involuntary infringement of copyright
has occurred, sincere apologies are offered, and the owners of
such copyright are requested to contact the publisher.

INDEX